What people are saying about
KRAV MIND

"Lori Farber's Krav Mind coupled with Dr. Neil Farber's superb contributions is a tour de force on successful life strategies, especially, when navigating adversity. Lori masterfully encapsulates the human mind's essential coping and resiliency stratagems including confidence, accountability, emotional regulation, self-discipline, and all-important peaceful conflict resolution among many others. I highly recommend this insightful, compelling book; a truly great addition to the Krav Maga world."

- **David Kahn, IKMA US Chief Instructor, Krav Maga Master Instructor, Bestselling Author**

"Many have asked me why I believe I have a successful career? My answer? I simply applied all the Martial Arts principles that I gathered over my life to whatever I like to pursue in life. It's SO refreshing to read a book that will actually talk about this?! I love it! Confidence, problem solving thinking, pushing your limits, discipline, self-control, communicating with others, dealing with stress, I can go on and on, it's all the same, it's crazy, and Lori Farber dives very deep into it so you know exactly what all the principles are. Really great!"

- **Bas Rutten, UFC Hall of Fame, Chairman Karate Combat, Inventor of the Bas O2 Trainer, Krav Maga Instructor**

"In Krav Mind, Lori Farber's wisdom shines through, offering readers a profound understanding of the symbiotic relationship between physical strength and mental resilience. An insightful read for those seeking personal growth through martial arts."

- **Moti Horenstein, Krav Maga Grandmaster, World Champion Fighter**

"Krav Mind is not just a book; it's a blueprint for mental empowerment. An essential read for anyone looking to sharpen their mind, build resilience, and thrive in all aspects of life. Krav Maga was developed and evolved through the lessons learned in real life challenges, and in turn the lessons found in Krav Maga, can be applied to all areas of life to overcome challenges and succeed."

- **Nir Maman, Counter Terror NCO, IDF Special Forces Counter Terror Unit**

"I'm a firm believer in the idea that martial arts — and especially Krav Maga — provide life skills beyond self defense. Lori Farber perfectly captures this idea in 'KRAV MIND'. Not only does she provide insightful commentary about the system itself, she underscores how easily Krav Maga training translates into other areas of your personal and professional growth. I highly recommend 'KRAV MIND' to anyone who wants to learn more about Krav Maga or about themselves!"

- **John Whitman, award winning author, 6th degree Black Belt in Krav Maga, Chief Instructor of Krav Maga Alliance.**

"Krav Maga has earned worldwide praise and respect for being a highly effective, well-integrated, no nonsense physical approach to self defense and fighting with specific applications for law-enforcement, military and security forces, as well as civilians. What makes the System so unique, is its approach to successfully deal with conflict and violence mentally, spiritually, emotionally and physically. You cannot be at your best to survive a violent encounter by only learning physical techniques. With excellence and thorough attention to the synergy that exists between the Krav Maga mind and body, Lori Farber has created a spectacular treatise on this often ignored side of Krav Maga. 'Krav Mind' equips you with the mental tools to develop the fighting spirit and emotional drive needed to survive violent street encounters. I fully recommend 'Krav Mind' as an addition to your Krav Maga library."

- **Darren Levine, Chief Instructor of Krav Maga Worldwide, LA County prosecutor, author, and entrepreneur**

"The art of self-defense has always required the art of self-mastery. Lori Farber's 'Krav Mind' is a roadmap to how the martial arts simultaneously trains the body and mind. Through increased mental fortitude, balance, discipline, calm, and resilience, the practitioner overcomes their inner fight while training for external threats. In everyday life, this is the most important victory of all. 'Krav Mind' will empower you to accomplish this."

- **Dr. Scott Maul, Physician, Top 100 Doctors, Instructor and Black Belts in Kavanah Krav Maga, Survival Hisardut and Combat Hapkido.**

"If the body may be compared to a fighter plane or a race car, then the mind should be trained to be the fighter pilot or the race car driver who manages that machine. The mind must run the body, not the opposite, especially during hardships, and definitely during combat and violent confrontation. Lori Farber's 'Krav Mind', brings you the insights and understanding of how proper Krav Maga training can help you achieve your highest potential on and off the mat. Improving and instilling courage, determination, controlled aggression, resilience, self-discipline, commitment, and personal growth requires an understanding of how to integrate the physical, technical and mental aspects of Krav Maga. Reading and contemplating on 'Krav Mind' will enrich you with the vast knowledge needed to do this. The next step is diligent practice."

- **Eyal Yanilov, President, Head Instructor, K.M.G. – Krav Maga Global, recipient of the *Founder's Diploma of Excellence* from Imi Lichtenfeld, author, electrical engineer.**

"A must read for anyone who practices Krav Maga. Lori Farber's 'Krav Mind' reflects on how the martial alignment of body, mind, and spirit creates a synergistic approach to life. Moving beyond the physical principles, while applying cognitive logos, and cultivating joy through the practical applications of empathy, gratitude, and empowerment. Truly an encouragement to embrace a martial journey to living with fullness."

- **Mark Gridley, Grandmaster Chon Tu Kwan Hapkido, Krav Maga Instructor, Founder of Tactical Pressure Point System**

KRAV MIND

**Mastering Fear and Building Confidence:
The Mental Edge of Krav Maga**

Copyright 2023 by Lori Farber
Dynamic Publishing Group
Phoenix, Arizona
info@theFIMA.com

eBook ISBN: 978-1-7361161-3-5
Paperback ISBN: 978-1-7361161-2-8
LCCN: #2023916744

All Right Reserved

No part of this book may be reproduced or transmitted in any form or by any means electronic or mechanical, including photocopying, recording, or by any information storage and retrieval system, without permission in writing from the publisher.

Printed in the United State of America

Disclaimer:

The practices, techniques, recommendations, and information provided in this book, "Krav Mind", are intended for general informational and educational purposes only. Nothing in this document constitutes any legal, medical, or professional opinion. While every effort has been made to ensure the accuracy and reliability of the content, the author and publisher do not assume any responsibility for errors, omissions, or outcomes based on the use of this information. This book should not be considered as a substitute for professional advice or guidance. Consult with qualified instructors, trainers, or healthcare professionals before attempting any physical or mental activities described in this book. The content is not intended to be a substitute for professional or legal advice. Always seek the advice of a legal professional with any questions or help you need regarding any of the topics provided, including legal use of force. Never disregard professional advice or delay in seeking it because of something you have read.

The reader assumes full responsibility for their actions and acknowledges that participation in any physical activities carries inherent risks. The author and publisher shall not be liable for any injuries, damages, or losses that may result from the use or misuse of the information provided in this book. By reading this book, the reader agrees to release the author and publisher from any and all claims, liabilities, or responsibilities arising from their use of the information presented herein

KRAV MIND

Mastering Fear and Building Confidence:
The Mental Edge of Krav Maga

BY LORI FARBER

Dynamic Publishing Group
Phoenix, Arizona

Table of Contents

DEDICATION 1

FOREWORD 3

ACKNOWLEDGEMENTS 5

CHAPTER 1: KRAV MIND 21

CHAPTER 2: ACCOUNTABILITY 29

CHAPTER 3: RESILIENCE 43

CHAPTER 4: CONFIDENCE 51

CHAPTER 5: FOCUS 59

CHAPTER 6: STRESS RELIEF 67

CHAPTER 7: DISCIPLINE AND SELF-CONTROL 73

CHAPTER 8: MINDFULNESS 83

CHAPTER 9: COMMUNICATION 93

CHAPTER 10: RELATIONSHIPS 105

CHAPTER 11: INTROSPECTION 117

CHAPTER 12: MIND-BODY CONNECTION 125

CHAPTER 13: EMBRACING FEAR 141

CHAPTER 14: VISUALIZATION 149

CHAPTER 15: EMPATHY 159

CHAPTER 16: EMOTIONAL REGULATION 167

CHAPTER 17: GRATITUDE 177

CHAPTER 18: LEADERSHIP 187

CHAPTER 19: EMPOWERMENT 197

CHAPTER 20: MENSCH ON A MAT 211

CHAPTER 21: KRAV WARRIOR MINDSET 221

CHAPTER 22: CONCLUSION 239

REFERENCES 253

ABOUT THE AUTHOR 289

Dedication

To my husband and best friend, Neil,

This book is dedicated to you, my guiding light and unwavering support. From the moment you introduced me to the world of martial arts and Krav Maga, my life transformed, and this newfound passion became an inseparable part of who I am today. Your belief in me and encouragement have been the driving force behind my personal journey to form a profound mind-body connection and experience a mental transformation like never before. Your patience and understanding during the countless hours I spent writing this book are a testament to your unconditional love and dedication. Your unwavering support has given me the strength and motivation to bring this work to fruition, and I am endlessly grateful.

Beyond our shared love for Krav Maga, you have been my constant companion, my confidant, and my pillar of strength. Your presence by my side has infused my life with boundless joy and inspiration. Together, we have embraced the challenges and celebrated the triumphs, reinforcing the power of unity and love in every endeavor.

To the entire FIMA family of Directors, Representatives, Instructors, and our cherished members, this book is dedicated to each one of you. The passion and dedication you bring to the world of Krav Maga are awe-inspiring, creating a supportive community that feels like home. Your commitment to personal growth and the mental benefits of Krav Maga have shaped the essence of this work, inspiring me to delve deeper into the power of the mind-body connection.

Your collective spirit has made FIMA not just an organization but a family - a family bound by the common thread of passion, resilience, and camaraderie. It is with deep affection that I extend my gratitude and love to you all.

To Neil and the entire FIMA family, thank you for enriching my life and inspiring the journey of Krav Mind and the Warrior Within. With love and heartfelt appreciation, this book is dedicated to each one of you. Together, we continue to grow, learn, and empower one another on this transformative quest.

Foreword

As a devoted student of Krav Maga, a certified life coach, and someone invested in the intricacies of human psychology, neurolinguistic programming (NLP), cognitive behavioral therapy (CBT), mindfulness, and visualization, my journey into the world of Krav Maga's mental benefits has been nothing short of transformative. I am a passionate advocate for unlocking the hidden power of Krav Maga's mind-body connection.

In my experience as the Director of FIMA – The Federation of Israeli Martial Arts, it became evident that while most practitioners of Krav Maga focused on its physical nature, the immense potential for mental growth and well-being had been largely overlooked. The profound psychological consequences I witnessed in myself, and my fellow practitioners compelled me to delve deeper into this unexplored territory.

As I explored the realms of emotional resilience, fear management, and heightened self-awareness fostered by Krav Maga, I realized that there was an important need to share these insights with the world. Surprisingly, there were few resources that addressed the invaluable mental benefits of Krav Maga.

In my role in FIMA, and after engaging in conversations with thousands of Krav Maga practitioners worldwide, the overwhelming consensus was undeniable: the mental health benefits of this dynamic art are monumental. It was particularly evident during the challenging times of the COVID pandemic when martial arts and self-defense schools faced closures. Krav Maga practitioners displayed extraordinary fortitude, resilience, and courage to persevere amidst the adversities.

It was during this time that the true depth of their strengths revealed itself - it was not a coincidence, but a result of the positive mental consequences cultivated through their Krav Maga training. The mental edge of Krav Maga manifested itself in their unwavering determination, composure under pressure, and adaptability to unforeseen challenges.

Through "Krav Mind" my earnest endeavor is to shed light on the profound mental benefits of Krav Maga, empowering practitioners to awaken the warrior within. By unraveling the mind-body connection, we not only fortify ourselves in self-defense but also embark on a journey of personal growth and mental mastery. In these pages, I'll explore the transformative power of synchronizing breath with movement, the art of mindfulness, visualization, and fear management. Together, we'll uncover the warrior's path that leads to emotional resilience, enhanced focus, and profound self-awareness, unleashing the full potential of the Krav Mind and the warrior residing within us all.

Acknowledgements

This book is a labor of love that would not have been possible without the unwavering support and guidance of my husband and best friend, Grandmaster Dr. Neil Farber. Neil's extensive knowledge of both Krav Maga and mental wellness has been a wellspring of inspiration throughout this journey. Neil's background as a Professor of Psychology and certifications in Cognitive Behavioral Therapy, Mindfulness, Neurolinguistic Programming, Hypnotherapy, and Master Life Coaching has enriched the depth and understanding of the mental aspects explored in this book. His writings, from Psychology Today articles to books on Krav Maga, martial arts, and self-help, have served as invaluable resources that have shaped this work. I am grateful for his enduring encouragement, even after losing much of his eyesight and no longer being able to write. His support allowed me to draw from his published and unpublished materials, elevating the richness of this book.

I wish to express my deepest appreciation to the dedicated team at FIMA - the Federation of Israeli Martial Arts. To the directors, representatives, instructors, and faithful members of FIMA, your passion and commitment to Krav Maga and its mental benefits have fueled the essence of this book. Your lengthy discussions on principles, philosophies, and concepts have been instrumental in shaping its content. I want to acknowledge the remarkable contributions of individuals who have shared their expertise and insights in Krav Maga as well as other martial arts. I'm going to list many names of whom I specifically (and alphabetically), give my heartfelt thanks and sincere appreciation. The description of each one of these individuals could easily take up a page or more. They are all highly accomplished and talented friends:

Billy Blanks - a FIMA celebrity, founder of world-famous Tae Bo system. Beyond his fitness legacy, Billy is a former World Champion in Karate and motivational speaker. He has also appeared in various films and television shows.

Amir Boaron - FIMA Associate Grappling Director, and hugely successful Head Coach of the Israeli BJJ team. Graduate of Wingate and owner of Soul Fighters in Israel, Amir's been awarded "Coach of the Year" and is an inspiration.

Jacov Bresler - FIMA Kapap Director for U.S.A. with Black Belts in a variety of martial arts styles. A former IDF veteran and straight-to-the-point instructor, who understands the intricacies of human reactions and biomechanics. A successful film producer, director, and fight choreographer. Jacov is a close friend and one of the most knowledgeable martial artist I know.

Keith Burregi - FIMA representative who's trained Krav Maga with Master John Whitman and Kavanah with Dr. Farber. He's a Police Officer, owns a Krav Maga and MMA school, with programs for abuse and assault victim, which are free of charge because he believes in the importance of the mission.

K. Ravenhawk Cain - FIMA representative, ordained Buddhist Priest, and JuJutsu Soke. Raven has spent a lifetime learning martial arts and combat tactics. He teaches Krav Maga and MMA, does life coaching, spiritual leadership and is the lead singer/songwriter for the rock band Sing String Revolver.

Art Camacho - FIMA celebrity, a writer, actor, award-winning film director, producer, and stuntman. His film *Assassin X* won 7 awards with AOF. He's directed Steven Seagal in *Half Past Dead* and Dolph Lundgren in *Dead Trigger* and host of *The Camacho Experiment*. Featured in many martial arts magazines, Art is a true rags to riches example of fortitude and positivity.

Alain Cohen - FIMA board member and Israel representative. 6th Dan Black Belt from Raphy Elgrissy and certified by Wingate. He was a member of the Wingate Teaching Team, an Air Marshall and Counter-Terror Instructor. Alain (KMF-AC) has many affiliates around the world. He's always on the move, and always makes time for his friends.

Joe Corley - FIMA Honorary Grandmaster Advisory Council. Icon in martial arts, won many national championships, and famous sports commentator. He has multiple Black Belts including in Krav Maga. Featured in many magazines, was Black Belt's Man of the Year. Joe is CEO of PKA Worldwide; a man of action, who's made a strong mind-body connection.

Brandon Davis - FIMA 4th Dan Black belt instructor as well as a Chuck Norris Black Belt. He's head Krav instructor for UFAF and an instructor in Kavanah. Someone who truly understands the deeper meaning of Krav Maga and has honed the art of making connections and strong relationships.

Cameron Davis – FIMA representative, excellent Kavanah and Krav Maga instructor. He was a security contractor for the Department of Homeland Security in addition to working in VIP and executive protection. Cameron is the Chief Instructor of Davis Martial & Fitness.

Shuki Drai - FIMA knife director, board member, IDF veteran and inventor of the SRT – Survival, Rescue Tool, used by law enforcement agencies. Shuki helps make Jewish institutions safer. He's an eclectic martial artist blending many styles seamlessly. Shuki is a kind-hearted man and an excellent instructor. His friendship is greatly appreciated.

Sara Eaglewoman - Revered spiritual healer, Urban Shaman, and Doctor of the Soul. She's adept in Shamanic Medicine, intuitive healing, and life counseling, guiding individuals towards self-realization. A consultant to Fortune 500 leaders and celebrities, Sara's beauty shines both inside and out."

Joseph Edmondson - FIMA representative and USA Chief Instructor Kavanah Krav Maga. He's a decorated martial artist, Halls of Fame inductee who's has won national championships in point and full-contact fighting. Joseph operates Krav Maga and BJJ schools in Arizona and works in VIP/EP security. He instructs with dedication and is a dear friend.

Maurice Elmalem – FIMA board member, professional artist, award-winning architect, holding many Black Belts. He's US Cup Gold Medalist, AAU Champion with 8 Guinness World Records. Maurice has written several books on martial arts and is the US Editor for BUDO magazine. He's been on television and film. A great friend and positive inspirational figure.

GM Moshe Galisko - FIMA Kapap Director, board member, developer of Modern Kapap. He's President of the International Kapap Association, Chairman of the Israeli and European Karate Association and Head of the Israeli Martial Arts Center. Moshe's a dear friend and wealth of knowledge about Kapap.

Prince Gharios - FIMA celebrity and Royal Highness. A direct disciple of Steven Seagal, as well as Yoshimitsu Yamada (disciple of Aikido founder Morihei Ueshiba). HRH has received many awards including the AOF Icon and International Sports Hall of Fame. He is a Humanitarian, author, actor, and artist whose mission is to promote peace and education.

GM Haim Gidon - FIMA Honorary Grandmaster Advisory Council, one of the first people in the world to receive a Black Belt in Krav Maga and one of only two people awarded an 8th Dan by Imi Lichtenfeld. He co-founded the Israeli Krav Maga Association and became president in 1994 upon Imi's retirement. Haim is a 10th Dan, decorated IDF veteran and tank operator who fought in the Six-Day War, the War of Attrition, and the Yom Kippur War. A true Krav Maga icon and wealth of knowledge about Krav Maga.

Dr. Itay Gil - FIMA Krav Maga and Military Organization Director, and board member. An IDF paratrooper, Yamam (counter-terror unit) member and instructor, director of training programs for Israel Border Police and founder of Protect Academy. Itay is a security expert featured on History Channel's "Human Weapons" and BBC's "Ultimate Hell Week." He's a close friend, knowledgeable about all things Krav Maga.

Sifu Alan Goldberg – board member, named 2004 Kung Fu Artist of the Year by Black Belt Magazine. He's an actor, producer, director, and developed Law Enforcement Survival Systems. The "Godfather of Martial Arts," is a dear friend and advisor, hosting the Hall of Honors Weekend annually in Atlantic City – The greatest event of its kind in the world.

Dr. Robert Goldman - FIMA board member, visionary and philanthropist. Holder of 20+ World Records, including 321 handstand pushups, his accomplishments, from awards like JFK Physical Fitness Award to Lifetime Achievement Award from Gov. Schwarzenegger. Dr. Bob founded the field of anti-aging medicine, International Sports Hall of Fame, certified personal training, and more. With two Medical Degrees, PhDs, he's an inspiration in martial arts and insight meditation. Dr. Bob is a cherished friend, role model, and beacon of wisdom and vitality.

Haim Gozali - FIMA's Grappling Director, board member, and Israel's top Gracie BJJ practitioner. A World Champion mixed martial artist, and catalyst for Bellator's Israel. He won, ADCC and Bareknuckle Championship, served in Israeli Border Police and survived a nightclub knife attack – a resilient warrior.

GM Mark Gridley - FIMA board member, Kavanah instructor, and Combat Hapkido Grandmaster. An excellent teacher with Instructor of the Year awards, Mark is Founder of the Tactical Pressure Points system and inducted into several Halls of Fame. Beyond martial arts, Mark is a nurse, Army veteran, and CEO of a large healthcare network. He is a genuine friend and definition of a mensch.

Noah Gross - FIMA celebrity, focusing on practical weapons, IDF veteran, Instructor at A.C.T. (Armed Combat and Tactics) and world-renowned specialist in historical European martial arts, Kapap and Krav Maga history. He's authored "Kapap from the Field to the Battlefield". Noah's an artist, life coach and psychotherapist, guiding individuals in overcoming grief, depression, anxiety, and PTSD, leading them towards mental health and wellness. He's a remarkable individual.

An-shu Stephen K. Hayes - FIMA Honorary Grandmaster Advisory Council, spent 15+ years training in Japan, Ninjutsu 10th Dan, and founded To-Shin Do. Former Dalai Lama bodyguard and according to Black Belt magazine, "One of the ten most influential martial arts masters alive." Ordained practitioner of Tendai Mikkyo Buddhism and a Buddhist priest, Stephen is an author, and respected, enlightened soul. Sir Stephen Hayes is one of the most interesting men in the world.

James Hiromasa - FIMA representative, life coach, and Expert on POST Committee for Arrest Control and Defensive Tactics. With his wife Shannon, their Krav Maga centers were awarded "Best in Colorado". James earned Senior Krav Maga Instructor status from Wingate in Israel. Author of the bestselling book, "How to be a Super Hero", offering practical tips on situational awareness, stress responses, and training techniques.

GM Hanshi Moti Horenstein - FIMA Co-Founder and President. Moti was picked to be FIMA President because Neil Farber wanted someone that everyone liked" – that's Moti. Israeli Special Forces veteran, first Israeli UFC fighter, World Champion in 5 different styles, World Oyama Champion, King's Cup Muay Thai World Champion, and World Record Holder for bat breaks with his shins. Chief Instructor of Moti Horenstein's Krav-Maga MMA. Moti is a true Warrior and Gentleman, one of the nicest, toughest people ever.

Tomer Israeli - FIMA board member and Director of SLETA – Security/Law Enforcement Training Assoc. Captain in the Israeli Special Forces who fought behind enemy lines in Lebanon. An Executive Protection Special Agents Leader at the Israeli embassy in Washington in the Secret Service, then founded *Israeli Tactical School*, for EP and counter-terror training. He's a good friend who loves what he does.

David Kahn - FIMA board member and Combatives (ICTA) Director. David is an amazing individual who has trained all five branches of the U.S. military, as well as Federal, State, and Local Law Enforcement agencies. He's U.S. Chief Instructor for

IKMA (Israeli Krav Maga Association), under GM Haim Gidon, a prolific writer on all things Krav Maga and has published 7 fantastic books about various aspects of Krav Maga. David has been an inspiration for this project.

Sifu Samuel Kwok - FIMA Honorary Grandmaster Advisory Council, Founder of Samuel Kwok Wing Chun with affiliates all over the world. He's an author, artist, Chi Gong energy healer, and renowned authority on Kung Fu. Sifu is one of my meditation partners, teacher, spiritual leader, and friend.

Laurian Lapadatu - FIMA representative, served in Romanian army, Tactical Firearms Combat Instructor, teaches VIP protection, hostage rescue, advanced driving, and arresting techniques. He has Black Belts in many styles, 4th Dan in Krav Maga and certified in 5 different Krav Maga organizations. He has a large, dedicated following, including myself.

Eric Lee - FIMA celebrity, actor, film director, and producer. He had roles in Rambo: First Blood Part II, and many other films. Eric is a World Champion – undefeated in Kata and weapons, winning over 100 titles. On the cover of many magazines and inducted into many Halls of Fame. Eric is a master of many things, from music to art to films. He has unleashed his inner Warrior and is a great source of inspiration.

Darren Levine – board member and Director of Krav Maga Committee. Trained at Wingate's first International Krav Maga Instructor Course, received a Black Belt and Founder Diploma from Imi Lichtenfeld. Darren is founder of Krav Maga Worldwide and responsible for spreading Krav Maga throughout the USA. He's deputy DA for LA County and lead prosecutor on a Crimes Against Peace Officers unit. Darren was one of the first Krav Maga instructors to employ meditation in classes and discuss using Krav Maga principles in business and life. Darren is a dear friend and source of support and positivity.

Carlos Machado - FIMA celebrity, pioneer of Brazilian Jiu Jitsu and former world master's champion. The Machado Method of teaching incorporates warm-ups, solo drills, partner drills, and flow rolling. Carlos has trained celebrities such as Chuck Norris and fighters, like Stephen "Wonderboy" Thompson. Carlos is a law school graduate, a quick-thinking man of action, dear friend, and a wealth of knowledge.

Nir Maman - FIMA Weapons Director and board member. Retired Sgt. Major from the IDF and lead counterterror and Krav Maga instructor for LOTAR. He's a sworn police constable and lead instructor in Tactical Training. He founded CT 707 training academy for security and law enforcement. Nir's a family man and Krav Warrior, externally and internally.

Dr. Scott Maul - FIMA Kavanah representative and longtime dedicated martial artist who spends time on the "inner arts" including a contemplative journey that began while living in Thailand. Scott is a Hematologist-Oncologist spending much of his time taking care of cancer patients. He is a giving person with mental fortitude and the resilience of a saint.

GM Guru Julius Melegrito - FIMA Blunt Weapons Director and Kavanah representative. A master of several martial arts, Black Belt in Krav Maga, feature of many magazines, and inducted into many Halls of Fame. Julius founded Philippine Martial Arts Alliance (PMAA) and contributed blunt weapon concepts to Kavanah. He's a certified Life Coach, dear friend, and a master at boiling things down to what matters.

Dr. Gregg Moral - FIMA Kavanah representative, marathon runner, elite tennis player and Krav Maga Black Belt. Gregg is a Navy Commander who brought Krav Maga to the Navy and

Marine base. As an interventional radiologist, Gregg's a critical thinker, who has focused on the mental aspects of Krav Maga.

Tommi Nystrom - FIMA representative, President of Finnish Krav Maga Federation, and someone who has looked deeply within Krav. Tommi was a military instructor in the Finnish Defense Forces and completed business school. He trains regularly in Israel and now focuses on education and how to accelerate skill acquisition in Krav Maga.

GM John Pellegrini - FIMA Honorary Grandmaster Advisory Council and Italian Armed Forces veteran. Founder of Combat Hapkido, the largest non-Korean founded Hapkido style. A grandmaster in many martial arts, author of best-selling books, inducted into every martial arts Hall of Fame and on the cover of many magazines. GMP is one of the most well-read people on the planet and has explored the martial applications of Yin/Yang. I appreciate our meaningful conversations.

GM Guy Rafaeli - FIMA board member and knife director. Trained in Krav Maga and Hisardut under Dennis Hanover, he was in military intelligence in the IDF, based in Lebanon. Specializing in CQB, Krav Maga, gun, knife, and baton. Guy became an IDF Krav Maga instructor and head instructor for Ultimate Krav Maga. He's an expert in all things bladed. Guy is a mensch and wealth of knowledge.

Master Ron Rotem - FIMA Krav Maga Director, board member and top Israeli Krav Maga instructor. His IDF service was in an Anti-Guerilla Unit. Head of the Krav Maga Section at the IDF, Israeli Prison System training, and the Israeli Krav Maga Institute in Israel. Admin of Krav Maga History and Culture FB group, Ron is an excellent Krav historian sharing knowledge with the international community.

Cynthia (Lady Dragon) Rothrock - FIMA celebrity, retired undefeated world champion with 100+ martial art wins, and holds 7 high level Black Belts. First woman on the cover of a martial arts magazine, inducted into many martial arts Hall of Fame, International Sports Hall of Fame, and Lifetime Achievement Award from Century Martial Arts. Cynthia has appeared in over 70 films and known for her high adventure world travels. She's a friend who lives life to the fullest.

Bruce Rubinberg - FIMA representative and FIMA Features Director. He won national and world fighting championships and is recognized for his strength, speed, sportsmanship, and fierceness. Inducted into several martial arts Halls of Fame for contributions to martial arts, he is a well-rounded, life-long martial artist who puts family first – and I love him for that.

Michael Ruppel – FIMA board member and former bodyguard for Jean-Claude van Damme. Michael is the Founder of Krav Maga Street Defence, teaching law enforcement, security, and military units all over the world. He's received international awards in martial arts and lives by the code of Krav Maga.

Chef Andre Rush - FIMA celebrity with degrees/certificates in Business, Culinary Sciences, Estate Management, and martial arts. A Master Sergeant in the U.S. Army, former White House Chef, and suicide prevention advocate, doing 2,222 pushups every day to support awareness of the 22 veterans who commit suicide every day. Andre is known for his enormous 24-inch biceps and his compassion.

Bas Rutten (El Guapo) - FIMA Board member and Director of International MMA Association. Bas is an amazing, deeply spiritual man. He's an actor (Here Comes the Boom), commentator, kickboxer, entrepreneur, inventor, coach and trainer,

World Champion Mixed Martial Artist, UFC Heavyweight Champion and Hall of Famer. He finished his fighting career on a 22-fight unbeaten streak, with 53 submissions. One of the most recognizable MMA faces in the sport, inventor of the Bas Body Action System and O2 Trainer, and Chairman for the Combat Karate Organization. Bas has a deep appreciation for Israel and is involved in teaching and promoting Krav Maga as a certified instructor. He's a great supporter of FIMA, a dear friend and source of inspiration.

Dan (The Beast) Severn - FIMA celebrity, UFC champion, trainer of UFC champions like Rashad Evans, Don Frye, and Quinton "Rampage" Jackson, and the only one to hold UFC and NWA championships at the same time. Dan's been featured in many magazines like USA Today and People and is one of 3 fighters with over *100 documented MMA wins*. He's an actor, motivational speaker, and co-host of the Toxic Masculinity podcast. Dan and his wife are close personal friends and I appreciate Dan's humor and stories.

Silvio Simac - FIMA celebrity, personal trainer, elite athlete, world champion martial artist, actor, stuntman, and fight choreographer. He's an adventure traveler, teacher, and businessman. Silvio's even performed on stage for Her Majesty the Queen! Inducted into many halls of fame and on several magazine covers, he's dedicated to helping others and raising money for charities like *Fighting for Cancer*. He trains in Krav Maga and supports FIMA's mission of supporting Israel. He is one of our meditation partners and I enjoy our conversations.

GM Jeff Smith - FIMA Honorary Grandmaster Advisory Council, rated #1-point fighter in the USA. He won the first Full Contact World Championships as a Light Heavyweight and made history winning the undercard for the Ali-Frazier fight.

He's a 10th degree Black Belt, inducted into every Hall of Fame, the first recipient of the Bruce Lee Award for Fighter of the Year and Joe Lewis Eternal Warrior Award. Jeff is the COO of Martial Arts Wealth Mastery and has positively influenced the lives of millions of martial artists around the world as a role model, teacher, mentor, coach, and leader. He's one of the nicest, most talented, and humble individuals I've ever known.

GM Jeff Speakman - FIMA Honorary Grandmaster Advisory Council and legend in martial arts, holding 10th degree in Kenpo and founder of the Kenpo 5.0 system. Perhaps best known for acting and lead role in *The Perfect Weapon*, he's received many awards, including Black Belt's Instructor of the Year and the ICON Award. Jeff exemplifies resilience! In 2013, diagnosed with throat cancer, he continued his work and passion in martial arts and teaching, eventually achieving a full recovery! He's very humble as he continues a path of self-development. He is an inspired, positive soul and motivational Guru.

Jesse James Tucker - FIMA representative, chief Instructor at Tucson's Rising Phoenix Self-Defense, and Fitness. An MMA fighter, with Black Belts in 4 different Krav Maga systems, he has trained champion grapplers, kickboxers, law enforcement, and military personnel. Jesse is a 4th Dan Black Belt in Kapap with GM Jacov Bresler and the FIMA Representative Liaison because of his excellent communication skills. He is a man who truly loves Krav and appreciates how it helps the community.

GM Benny (the Jet) Urquidez - FIMA celebrity member, held 6 world titles in 5 different weight divisions and finished his career with a record of 63-0. He was a pioneer of full-contact fighting and one of the best kickboxers in history, inducted into many Halls of Fame including the International Sports Hall of

Fame. Benny's students include David Lee Roth, John Cusack, and Patrick Swayze. He's authored several books, videos, and appeared in many films including *Spider-Man* and *Roadhouse*. Benny's explored the inner workings of martial arts and taken time for meaningful introspection. We've had many conversations about life and insights.

Ron Van Clief - FIMA celebrity - who survived a hanging by racists and getting shot down in Viet Nam. He was a Police Officer and World Championship martial artist who Bruce Lee called "The Black Dragon". Ron worked in over 300 movies and TV shows as an actor, stuntman, and action director. The oldest person to fight in UFC and at age 60, won a National Karate Championship. At 80 years young he's a brown belt in BJJ. Author of many books, screenplays, recipient of multiple awards including International Sports Hall of Fame and featured in many magazines, including, Sports Illustrated. Ron is one of the most resilient men in the world and his life story is inspiring.

Bill (Superfoot) Wallace - FIMA celebrity, World Full-Contact Middleweight Champion for 6 years, retiring undefeated at 23-0! He has degrees in Physical Education and a master's degree in Kinesiology. A US Air Force veteran, author, teacher, and actor, appearing in several movies with Jackie Chan, Chuck Norris, John Belushi and Mickey Rourke. Bill was the first UFC commentator and personal trainer and bodyguard for Elvis Presley and John Belushi. One of the best fighters in the world who embodies the qualities of resilience, fortitude, creativity, adaptability, optimism, and lots of humor. Always great conversations with Bill – my dance partner.

Gary Wasniewski - FIMA Honorary Grandmaster Advisory Council, grandmaster in several styles and founder of TYGA Karate with thousands of members. Gary has earned about every award and title in martial arts. He's a World Martial Arts Champion fighter, film director, producer, and classically trained actor, with advanced degrees in law and computer science. He founded the London International Hall of Fame, which donates all proceeds to cancer research – an example of how Gary is a real-life hero.

John Whitman - FIMA board member and representative, 6th degree black belt in Krav Maga, Sport Performance Coach and founder of Krav Maga Alliance. He's trained thousands of civilians and hundreds of law enforcement and military personnel. Author or co-author of foundational Krav Maga books and named in Black Belt as one of the seven martial artists "Defining the new standard for the 21st century." John's appeared in numerous media, including Today Show, ABC News, and CNN. He's a great friend, a true renaissance man, and a literary genius who's created several best-selling novels.

Don (The Dragon) Wilson - FIMA celebrity who won 11 World Titles in four different weight divisions. His kickboxing career lasted 4 decades, and it's been said that he's "Perhaps the greatest kickboxer in American history." Don's been in over 60 films and television shows, including: *The Expendables*, *Bloodfist*, *Batman Forever*, and *The Scorpion King*. He's been inducted into the International Sports Hall of Fame and featured in many magazines. Don is a man with great integrity and one of the most engaging people I know.

Eyal Yanilov - FIMA celebrity, graduate of Wingate, he studied Krav Maga with Imi Lichtenfeld beginning in 1974. Eyal was one of two people given the "Founder's Diploma of Excellence". He was an instructor at the 1st international instructor training camp in Israel (1981) and directed the first Krav Maga training seminar outside Israel. Eyal was the driving force for popularizing Krav Maga outside of Israel in the 1990s, co-founder of IKMF and then Krav Maga Global (KMG) for which he is the Chief Instructor. Eyal was featured on Human Weapon. He's one of the most recognized names in the world of Krav Maga, a good friend and wealth of knowledge about the system, its history, strategies, techniques, and principles.

To those whose names I may have inadvertently omitted, rest assured that your contributions are equally valued, and you will be rightfully acknowledged in future updates of this book. Your support has been a driving force, and this work would not have been possible without you.

To my husband, Neil, and the entire FIMA family, thank you for being my source of knowledge, insight, and inspiration.

CHAPTER 1

Krav Mind

Welcome to the exciting world of Krav Maga! This book will take you on a journey beyond just physical self-defense. We will explore the incredible mental benefits of this system and how it can transform your overall well-being and personal growth.

Krav Maga, originally from Israel, has become famous worldwide as a self-defense method used by military and law enforcement agencies. But it's not just for professionals! People from all walks of life are embracing Krav Maga as a means of self-defense and as a pathway to personal development.

The number of Krav Maga practitioners is growing rapidly, with schools and training centers popping up all over the world. People of all ages, backgrounds, and fitness levels are joining this ever-expanding community. This is a clear indication of the system's effectiveness and the desire for individuals to be prepared in today's unpredictable world.

As we venture into the mental benefits of Krav Maga, let's first understand its roots. In the early 1900s before Israel became an independent state and was ruled by the Turks and then the British, the Jews of Palestine had a need to protect themselves against local Arab and Bedouin tribes. They developed a group of freedom fighters called the Haganah and an underground paramilitary wing called Palmach. Starting in 1940, the Palmach taught a self-defense system called Kapap, an acronym for Krav Panim El Panim or "Face-to-face fighting. Kapap consisted of a collection of styles like boxing, wrestling, jiu jitsu, knife fighting, long and short stick, etc. These sections were each taught independently by specialists in those areas. Starting in 1948, when British Mandate Palestine became Israel, the Haganah essentially became the IDF (Israeli Defense Forces) and the Palmach essentially became the Israeli Special Forces. Most of the people in charge continued in the same roles. Kapap continued to be taught and practiced as the self-defense system of the IDF. In 1948, the term Krav Maga, which means "Contact Combat" was first introduced. Krav Maga referred to the same (and only) self-defense system used by the IDF. In the 1950s the terms Krav Maga and Kapap were used interchangeably. Imi Lichtenfeld, who immigrated to British Mandate Palestine from Bratislava in 1942, became a Kapap instructor and rose in rank and responsibility to become the Head Kapap and then Head Krav Maga instructor in the IDF. Imi became Head of the IDF's Krav Maga Division, where he further refined and expanded the system, melding the individual disciplines of Kapap into one cohesive system during the late 1950s for use in the IDF. When Imi Lichtenfeld retired from the IDF in the early 1960s he adapted Krav Maga for civilian use, popularizing it as a self-defense system accessible to everyone. Indeed, Imi Lichtenfeld, referred to as the Founder of Krav Maga, is the single most influential person in developing what we now know as Krav Maga. He started the first international Krav Maga organization and is responsible for introducing Krav Maga to the world outside of Israel.

Integral to Krav Maga are its guiding principles, which extend not only to physical techniques but also carry profound implications for the mental realm. These principles are very well laid out in the books referenced for this chapter by Darren Levine, David Kahn, John Whitman, Eyal Yanilov, Alain Cohen, and others. There are indeed some differences between the systems they represent, or as David Kahn is famous for saying, "Because not all Krav Maga is the same," (which is why FIMA exists, as a "better business bureau for Krav Maga"). However, all these high-level instructors and high-quality systems, do teach the same basic foundational principles as outlined below. In addition, David Kahn's "6 pillars of Krav Maga" from a Tactical perspective in the Israeli Krav Maga Association under Haim Gidon, are the same as the first six principles listed below.

1. **Simultaneous defense and counterattack**: Rather than practice blocking and counterstriking in sequence as done in many martial arts, Krav Maga engages in simultaneous (or nearly simultaneous) defensive and offensive movements. This relates to life outside of the dojo where we shouldn't procrastinate once we recognize imminent danger.
2. **Continuous Motion or Retzev**: Staying mobile and evasive during conflict aligns with mental adaptability and embracing change.
3. **Reflexive Response**: Krav Maga trains practitioners to respond quickly and decisively, encouraging mental resilience and adaptability in coping with challenges,

whether they be against a violent attack or an important life decision. The most efficient way to deliver reflexive responses is to make sure that these techniques optimize your body's natural, instinctive motions. In doing so, you are more likely to be able to yield maximum speed and power.
4. **Focus on vulnerabilities:** Knowing vulnerable targets both yours and your opponent's is critical to staying safe and to ending a confrontation quickly. It invokes the Pareto principle that 80% of your effect will come from 20% of your actions. In all aspects of life, defending yourself, at home, or on the job, make every action count.
5. **Simplicity**: Krav Maga focuses on simple, instinctive techniques, fostering a straightforward approach to problem-solving and decision-making in both physical and mental domains. Build upon these elemental techniques as you master each. This principle can be applied to any new skill, language, or hobby.
6. **Threat Neutralization**: The primary goal is to neutralize threats swiftly. Use subduing techniques to de-escalate situations quickly. This mirrors mental adeptness in addressing negative thoughts or emotions promptly.
7. **Training for Reality**: Techniques trained in realistic scenarios prepare practitioners mentally for real-life challenges and stressors, building resilience, and overcoming fight paralysis.
8. **Visualization**: Incorporating visualization into your training on the mat and in other aspects of your life, improves your ability to anticipate obstacles and rise to challenges.

9. **Situational Awareness:** Using mindfulness and situational awareness to recognize and analyze potential threats, including reading non-verbal cues and body language. This also involves being aware of your environment, including obstacles such as nearby vehicles, furniture, walls, curbs, sloped or rough ground, ice or slippery floors, etc. In this way you may be able to utilize pre-emptive strikes or avoid or evade confrontations.
10. **Aggression**: Emphasizing proactive and assertive action in self-defense, Krav Maga fosters a mindset for overcoming mental obstacles and pursuing personal growth. Understanding that in physical confrontations, you will experience stress, excitement, fear, and a huge surge of adrenaline.
11. **Efficiency**: Every move aims to achieve the desired effect with minimal energy and time, echoing mental efficiency in better focus, attention management, and productivity.
12. **Economy of Motion**: Avoiding unnecessary movements conserves energy physically and mentally by being mindful of thoughts and emotions.
13. **Multiple Points of Attack**: Attacking multiple targets simultaneously reflects multitasking and effective management of various life aspects.
14. **Controlled Aggression**: Directing aggression towards the threat applies mentally as well, channeling emotions constructively and not letting them control actions.
15. **Multiple Attackers**: Always assume that your attacker is not alone. Prepare both mentally and physically for

the potential of having to confront multiple assailants. When you have this mentality, you will be more likely to avoid going to the ground and to try to "take the back" and get to the dead side.

Krav Maga is extremely effective when it comes to self-defense, but its benefits go beyond just physical techniques. The mental advantages are just as profound. By training in Krav Maga, individuals can discover their inner strength and resilience. They learn to overcome fears, embrace personal growth, and become independent individuals who believe in their own abilities. One of the core principles of Krav Maga is reality-based training, where practitioners are exposed to extreme conditions to test their skills. Dr. Itay Gil is a prime example of a Krav Maga master who ensures that everything he teaches can be performed under stress. The mental benefits of Krav Maga don't stop there. The practice fosters discipline and self-control, providing a framework for managing emotions, making rational decisions, and developing a strong sense of personal responsibility. The principles and values instilled through Krav Maga training seamlessly translate into other areas of life, contributing to personal and professional success.

In today's busy world, it's more important than ever to have mental strength and confidence. Krav Maga can give you these qualities. This martial art/self-defense system teaches you to embrace and overcome obstacles, making you mentally tough and resilient. The benefits of Krav Maga go beyond self-defense. It boosts your belief in yourself and your ability to handle tough situations. This newfound confidence extends to all areas of your life, improving your self-esteem and giving you a sense of control.

Krav Maga also improves your focus, awareness, and decision-making skills. The intense training keeps you fully engaged and aware of your surroundings. This heightened level of awareness carries over to everyday life, helping you handle challenges with a clear mind and quick responses.

In addition to the individual benefits, Krav Maga builds a sense of community and camaraderie among practitioners. The shared experiences, partner drills, and mutual support create a supportive and inclusive environment where relationships are nurtured, trust is fostered, and teamwork is celebrated. Within the Krav Maga community, you find a network of like-minded individuals who share a common passion for personal growth, self-defense, and mental well-being.

While physical fitness is undoubtedly a significant aspect of a healthy lifestyle, mental well-being is equally important. Krav Maga offers a unique avenue to cultivate mental resilience, emotional stability, and a positive mindset.

Throughout the following chapters, we'll delve into the various aspects of Krav Maga that contribute to mental well-being. We'll explore the practices of accountability, confidence building, focus, discipline, empowerment, introspection, communication, resilience, stress relief, mindfulness, relationships, mind-body connection, and more. Each chapter will provide insights, strategies, and practical tips to harness the mental benefits of Krav Maga and apply them to your daily life.

It is my hope that by the end of this book, you will have gained a profound understanding of the transformative power of Krav Maga beyond its physical aspects and appreciate Krav Maga's holistic approach to personal development, mental fortitude, and overall well-being.

CHAPTER 2

Accountability

"Krav training hones not just our physical skills, but our mental strength, where accountability serves as the bridge between intention and achievement."

Dr. GM Neil Farber

In this chapter, we explore how accountability plays a crucial role in Krav Maga training. By understanding its importance and taking responsibility, we can develop this essential quality. We also discover how accountability has positive effects on our mental well-being and how it empowers us to succeed in all areas of life, beyond just training.

Understanding Accountability and Responsibility

At the heart of personal growth and positive mindset lies a powerful duo: accountability and responsibility. Success gurus Stephen Covey and Dr. Neil Farber both emphasize the importance of these qualities in their books. Covey's 7 *Habits of Highly Effective People*, places accountability as the first habit to realizing success, while Farber's, *Throw Away Your Vision Board* designates responsibility as the first Key to

Achievement. Understanding these principles is the key to achieving a fulfilling and purposeful life.

Contrary to what many believe, being accountable and responsible is not a heavy burden or a way to restrict ourselves. In fact, it signifies maturity and empowerment. Embracing accountability means taking ownership of our actions, decisions, and the results they bring. Instead of deflecting blame or making excuses, accountable individuals admit their role in shaping their destinies. They actively seek to make things right when needed. This sense of responsibility liberates us from the constraints of being victims and gives us the power to take charge of our own lives.

In Krav Maga training, accountability is crucial. It means that you are responsible for your progress and success. Every technique you learn and every skill you improve on shows your dedication and determination. This mindset pushes you to constantly improve yourself and become a master of self-defense. By admitting your weaknesses and working hard to overcome them, you become resilient and develop a mindset of growth that goes beyond the training mat.

> *"With accountability as our ally, the Krav Mind unleashes the potential for greatness, transforming us into masters of our own destiny."*

Being accountable isn't just important in martial arts, it's also crucial in professional settings. When we take ownership of our tasks and responsibilities, it makes us reliable and trustworthy team members. This leads to consistent results and upholding our commitments, earning the respect and admiration of our colleagues and superiors. In personal relationships, accountability builds trust and harmony by emphasizing open communication and considering how our actions affect others. By holding ourselves accountable for our emotions and reactions, we create healthier connections and handle conflicts with empathy and understanding.

Understanding and embracing accountability and responsibility lays the foundation for personal growth, positive mindsets, and fulfilling relationships. This mindset doesn't just benefit us in Krav Maga, but applies to every aspect of our lives. By being accountable, we can face challenges with determination, learn from setbacks, and pursue a path of purpose and fulfillment.

Forging Accountability through Krav Maga Training

Krav Maga training is a powerful tool for developing accountability and responsibility in all aspects of your life. The challenging and rigorous nature of the training pushes you to grow and improve yourself, and accountability becomes a guiding force on your journey.

Instructors play a pivotal role in fostering accountability, but it ultimately comes down to you to internalize and apply the lessons learned. By taking ownership of your training, setting goals, and working diligently to achieve them, you become an active participant in your self-defense journey.

> *"Krav Maga warriors understand that true strength lies in taking responsibility, a powerful truth that liberates us to become architects of our own success."*

Krav Maga's practicality and real-world focus also reinforce accountability. You understand that the techniques you learn aren't just for show, but essential skills that could be needed in self-defense situations. This understanding highlights your responsibility to sharpen your abilities, ensuring that you're well-prepared to protect yourself and others when necessary.

With its focus on goal setting, discipline, consistency, and personal safety, Krav Maga training offers a comprehensive approach to self-improvement and empowerment. By fostering accountability and awareness, it equips you with skills and mindset to navigate life's challenges confidently and safely.

Achieving Goals: In the world of self-defense, Krav Maga training provides a unique approach to goal setting and follow-through. By setting specific and realistic objectives, such as mastering a technique, earning a higher rank, or improving endurance, you are able to track your progress and hold yourself accountable. This discipline and dedication fostered through Krav Maga training enables you to stay committed even in the face of challenges and obstacles.

Consistency: Regular attendance at classes creates a sense of accountability to oneself and to training partners. This commitment to consistent practice strengthens your sense of responsibility, ensuring continuous effort is invested in improving skills.

Personal Safety Awareness: By developing situational awareness and taking responsibility for your own protection, you become more conscious of potential threats and dangers in your environment. This heightened awareness extends beyond self-defense, translating into making safer choices in various areas of life.

Constructive Feedback: In Krav Maga, instructors and training partners give you helpful feedback to make your techniques and performance better. When you accept and use this feedback, you show that you're responsible for your own learning and growth. Feedback is a crucial step toward improvement.

Safety in Training: When you practice with a partner or in sparring, it's very important to consider the safety and well-being of your training partners. You need to take responsibility for your actions and make sure you are practicing with control and respect. This responsibility helps create a safe and supportive training environment for everyone in the Krav Maga community.

Training Ethos: To fully embrace Krav Maga, you need to have a mindset of always wanting to get better and pushing yourself to do more. It's about stepping out of your comfort zone and taking on challenging tasks. This shows that you are accountable for your own personal growth and development.

Krav Maga training helps you become more accountable and teaches valuable life skills. It goes beyond just martial arts and can have a positive impact on all aspects of your life. By being responsible and taking ownership of your actions, you become better equipped to face challenges and achieve your goals. This mindset of accountability leads to personal empowerment and success. You can apply these principles in your personal relationships, professional endeavors, and pursuit of personal goals. Embracing accountability allows you to be proactive and find solutions instead of dwelling on problems.

Through the challenges and triumphs of Krav Maga training, you forge a deep-rooted sense of accountability that becomes an integral part of your character. This cultivated accountability not only strengthens your performance in self-defense but enriches your life as you navigate challenges with resilience, courage, and a commitment to continuous growth. The transformative power of Krav Maga lies not just in mastering self-defense techniques but in shaping you into an accountable, empowered, and purpose-driven warrior both on and off the training mat.

The Mental Health Benefits of Responsibility

Krav Maga training can have a tremendous impact on your mental health and well-being. By taking ownership and being responsible for your actions, you can develop a positive mindset that positively affects every aspect of your life. The benefits for your mental health are truly remarkable.

"Beyond physical prowess, Krav Maga empowers us with the mental prowess of responsibility, where every step forward becomes a testament to our commitment."

Reduced Stress and Anxiety: Taking responsibility for your actions and choices gives you control over what you can control. When you understand that your decisions and efforts can influence outcomes, you feel less stressed and anxious about things you can't control. Being able to handle challenges calmly allows you to better deal with difficult situations.

Increased Resilience: Embracing responsibility makes you more resilient, meaning you can bounce back from tough times. When you see setbacks and failures as opportunities for growth, you have a positive outlook on challenges. This mindset helps you keep going during hard times, learning from your experiences and coming out stronger and more determined.

Enhanced Self-Efficacy: Responsibility builds your self-belief, the confidence in your abilities to achieve your goals. As you see yourself making progress and succeeding through hard work, you gain confidence in overcoming obstacles in other areas of life. This newfound self-belief empowers you to take on new challenges with optimism and determination.

Improved Self-Image: Accountability reinforces a positive self-image. When you take responsibility for your actions, you develop integrity and self-respect. This self-awareness and honesty contribute to a positive self-concept, leading to increased self-esteem and a greater sense of worthiness.

Improved Problem-Solving Skills: Taking responsibility helps to develop your problem-solving abilities. In Krav Maga training, you are presented with different situations that require you to think quickly and make effective decisions. By applying this mindset to real-life scenarios, you become skilled at analyzing challenges and finding helpful solutions.

Stronger Relationships: Having a sense of responsibility in your interactions with others leads to healthier and more satisfying relationships. When you take ownership of your behavior, communication, and actions, you contribute to an environment of trust and respect in both personal and professional relationships.

Increased Motivation and Goal Achievement: Being accountable for your actions provides the drive to set and accomplish goals. As you see the positive results of your efforts in Krav Maga, you become more motivated to pursue other aspirations in life. By holding yourself accountable to your objectives, you maintain commitment and focus on achieving your desired outcomes.

Greater Emotional Regulation: Responsibility helps you develop emotional regulation skills. As you take ownership of your emotions and responses, you learn to manage stress and frustrations effectively. This ability to control emotions positively impacts your mental and emotional well-being.

Sense of Purpose: Embracing accountability gives your life a sense of purpose and direction. When you understand the impact of your choices and actions, you become more intentional in your pursuits, leading to a more fulfilling and meaningful life.

Empowerment and Autonomy: Accountability empowers you to take control of your life. As you recognize that you hold the reins of your destiny, you become more self-reliant and autonomous, capable of making empowered decisions for yourself.

Cultivating a positive mindset through responsibility in Krav Maga training sets the foundation for improved mental health and overall well-being. By embracing accountability, you harness the power to navigate life's challenges with resilience, optimism, and purpose, enriching both your martial arts journey and your personal growth. As you build a Krav Warrior Mindset centered around responsibility, you unlock the mental edge that propels you to thrive in all aspects of life.

Thriving in All Aspects of Life

Through your Krav Maga training, you develop a strong sense of accountability that goes beyond just the training mat. This newfound sense of responsibility empowers you to excel in all areas of life. As you incorporate these principles into different aspects of your life, you'll undergo positive changes that contribute to personal growth and achievement.

> *"The Krav Mind embraces accountability, recognizing that progress is born from accepting responsibility for our choices, both on and off the training mat."*

Professional Life: In the workplace, you're responsible and dependable. You take ownership of your tasks, meet deadlines, and strive for excellence. You're proactive in solving problems and work well with others, which helps build a positive reputation and opens doors for career growth and opportunities.

Time Management: You have excellent time management skills, which allow you to efficiently divide your time between work, training, and personal commitments. By prioritizing tasks and setting clear goals, you maximize productivity and successfully achieve your objectives.

Academic Pursuits: You demonstrate accountability in your studies, Krav Maga and others. You dedicate time to learning, seek assistance when needed, and thoroughly prepare for exams. This sense of responsibility translates into improved academic performance and a deeper love for learning.

Health and Fitness: When you embrace accountability in your fitness journey, you commit to sticking to your training routines, maintaining a balanced diet, and prioritizing self-care. By doing this, you'll experience improved physical and mental well-being, which will have a positive impact on your overall quality of life.

Financial Responsibility: When you take accountability for your financial decisions, create a budget, and plan for the long-term, you're setting yourself up for financial success. By setting goals, saving wisely, and avoiding impulsive spending, you'll achieve greater financial security and stability.

Family and Relationships: Accountability is key to strong communication and trust in your personal relationships. By taking responsibility for your actions, being willing to apologize when necessary, and actively working to resolve conflicts in a constructive way, you'll foster deeper connections, create a supportive family environment, and strengthen bonds with your loved ones.

Personal Growth: You have a strong desire to improve yourself and constantly seek out opportunities to do so. This includes attending workshops, obtaining certifications, and participating in personal development activities. By investing in your own growth, you'll reach your full potential, expand your skills, and discover new passions.

Giving Back: You feel a sense of duty towards your community and actively contribute to it through volunteering, supporting charitable causes, and getting involved in local initiatives. Being an agent of positive change, you'll inspire others to make a difference and create a more vibrant community.

Achieving Goals: In various aspects of your life, you set ambitious yet attainable goals. You break these goals down into smaller, manageable steps, celebrating milestones along the way and staying focused on your objectives. Through dedication and accountability, you know that success is within reach, whether it's mastering advanced self-defense techniques, earning a degree, or starting your own business.

Emotional Regulation: Taking responsibility helps you control your emotions in personal interactions. You learn to respond to difficult situations with empathy, understanding, and constructive communication. This leads to better relationships and resolving conflicts using emotional intelligence.

Stress Management: Embracing accountability in managing stress means finding healthy ways to cope and practicing mindfulness. It reduces stress, improves mental clarity, and helps you stay composed in challenging situations.

Personal Safety: The accountability you learn in Krav Maga training also applies to personal safety in everyday life. You become more vigilant, make safe choices, and avoid risky situations. This increased awareness improves your well-being and the well-being of those around you.

Conclusion

The importance of accountability in a powerful Krav Warrior Mindset goes beyond physical strength. Through Krav Maga training, challenging techniques, and supportive instructors, you develop a strong sense of responsibility that extends beyond self-defense. This mindset brings mental health benefits like improved emotional control, increased self-confidence, and better stress management. Taking responsibility and setting goals in Krav Maga not only improves martial arts skills but also helps you succeed in all areas of life.

When you incorporate accountability into every aspect of your life, your Krav Maga journey becomes a catalyst for personal growth and well-being. You become a confident individual who faces challenges with determination and resilience. This mindset has a positive impact on your personal and professional life, enabling you to thrive in whatever you pursue.

CHAPTER 3

Resilience

"Krav Maga teaches us that resilience isn't just a skill, but a state of mind, allowing us to rise from the ashes of defeat and soar to new heights."

Dr. GM Neil Farber

Resilience is crucial for our mental well-being, allowing us to navigate tough times and emerge stronger. In the world of Krav Maga, resilience is more than just physical strength; it includes mental toughness too. By undergoing challenging training, you develop resilience that permeates all areas of your life. In this chapter, we'll see how Krav Maga fosters resilience, why it's important to embrace adversity, and how overcoming obstacles can lead to personal growth and exceeding our limits.

Developing Mental Toughness through Challenging Training

Krav Maga training is known for its intense and demanding nature, both physically and mentally. While physical fitness is important, the mental aspect is just as crucial. Krav Maga pushes you to tap into your inner strength, teaching you to overcome challenges and persevere. Through consistent practice and exposure to difficult scenarios, you develop mental toughness, resilience, and the ability to stay focused under pressure.

> *"The resilience cultivated in Krav Maga is a powerful armor, protecting us from doubt and fear, enabling us to conquer any obstacle that stands in our way."*

In Krav Maga, techniques are designed to simulate real-life encounters, placing you in scenarios that test your mental fortitude. By continuously pushing your limits and stepping outside your comfort zone, you learn to adapt, problem-solve, and respond effectively even in high-stress situations. Dr. Itay Gil, a Krav Maga instructor from the Yamam – Israel's National Counter Terror Unit, focuses less on specific techniques and more on making sure that you are pushed to and beyond your comfort zone to develop the resilience necessary for real-world encounters. Dr. Gil has co-authored (with Dr. Neil Farber) two articles in Psychology Today about resilience. The first (Resilience: The Ultimate Stress Test) focuses on how highly resilient recruits were selected for service in elite special forces. The second article (Failing Your Way to Success) discusses how to specifically transform stress into resilience and develop internal strength through visualization, goal-setting, repetitive training to failure, and finally communication with adequate debriefing for stress-response management.

Embracing Adversity and Bouncing Back Stronger

In Krav Maga, adversity which is an inevitable part of life, should be embraced as an opportunity for growth. In training, you are exposed to various challenges, including physical exhaustion, simulated attacks, and situations that require quick thinking. By facing these adversities, you build resilience, and learn to overcome obstacles instead of avoiding them.

> *"In the face of adversity, a Krav Maga warrior rises like a Phoenix, harnessing the power of resilience to emerge stronger and more tenacious."*

Krav Maga also teaches you to see setbacks as learning opportunities rather than failures. Every moment of adversity becomes an opportunity for growth and self-improvement. With this mindset, individuals become stronger and more resilient, ready to face of future challenges. The ability to embrace adversity is a valuable life skill that goes beyond the training mat, empowering individuals to handle tough situations with confidence and determination.

Overcoming Obstacles and Pushing Beyond Limits

As Darren Levine has written, altercations actually involve two fights: one with your opponent and one with yourself. Krav Maga training often pushes individuals beyond what they initially believed were their limits. By challenging and surpassing these limits, you discover your true potential and realize that you can achieve more than you once thought possible. This process of overcoming obstacles and pushing beyond limits fosters a sense of empowerment and self-belief that can positively impact all aspects of life.

Krav Maga techniques require you to push your physical and mental boundaries, pushing through fatigue, discomfort, and fear. As your skills and techniques improve, you build confidence in your ability to overcome challenges. This newfound confidence influences how you approach obstacles in your personal and professional lives.

> *"Pushing beyond physical and mental limits in Krav Maga builds an unbreakable spirit, one that thrives on the challenges life throws our way."*

By consistently pushing beyond your perceived limits in training, you develop resilience that enables you to tackle challenges head-on. You learn to embrace discomfort, confront fears, and persevere even when faced with difficult circumstances.

Resilience Off the Mat: Thriving in All Aspects of Life

Resilience cultivated through Krav Maga training extends far beyond the training mat. In everyday life, the mental toughness and adaptability honed in Krav Maga become powerful tools for handling various challenges and thriving in different situations.

> *"Beyond the training mat, the resilience nurtured in Krav Maga permeates all aspects of life, empowering us to face anything that comes our way with unshakable resolve."*

Work and Career: Resilience allows you to navigate workplace challenges with grace and composure. You're better equipped to handle high-pressure situations, difficult coworkers, or setbacks, leading to improved problem-solving skills and productivity.

Relationships: The ability to bounce back from conflicts and misunderstandings strengthens your emotional resilience, leading to healthier and more fulfilling relationships. Resilience helps you communicate effectively and maintain positive connections with others, fostering a supportive social network.

Health and Wellness: Mental resilience positively impacts your overall well-being. You become more likely to persevere in pursuing health goals, like maintaining regular exercise routines or making healthier lifestyle choices.

Personal Growth: Resilience fuels personal development, allowing you to embrace challenges as opportunities for learning and growth. You're more open to trying new experiences and stepping out of your comfort zone, leading to self-discovery and continuous improvement.

Decision-making: Mental toughness enables you to make rational decisions even in difficult situations. You stay focused and composed when facing tough choices, minimizing impulsive reactions and promoting better judgment.

Adapting to Change: Life is full of unexpected twists and turns. Resilience helps you handle changes and uncertainties, promoting adaptability and flexibility in the face of life's unpredictability.

Stress Management: Mental resilience aids in managing stress effectively. Better coping mechanisms allow you to handle stressors in a healthy manner, reducing the negative impact of chronic stress on your mental and physical well-being.

Goal Achievement: Resilience drives you to stay committed to your goals despite setbacks or obstacles. You become more persistent in pursuing your aspirations, increasing the likelihood of achieving success.

Confidence and Self-esteem: As you demonstrate resilience in various areas of life, your self-confidence and self-esteem grow. You gain a deep sense of self-assurance, knowing you can handle challenges and emerge stronger from difficult situations.

Community Leadership: Mentally resilient individuals often become beacons of strength and inspiration. Your ability to overcome challenges can positively influence and motivate others to develop their resilience and face adversity with courage.

By embracing resilience as a core value in both your Krav Maga training and everyday life, you develop a powerful mindset that empowers you to tackle challenges with unwavering determination and an unyielding spirit. The mental toughness honed through Krav Maga serves as a catalyst for personal growth, success, and well-being in all facets of life.

Conclusion

Resilience is a key quality in Krav Maga that can transform your life. Through tough training and challenging situations, you develop both physical endurance and mental strength. Facing adversity and bouncing back become second nature, helping you succeed in all areas of life.

The mental resilience you gain from Krav Maga affects how you approach challenges, relationships, and personal growth. By pushing past your limits and embracing discomfort, you build unwavering confidence in your ability to overcome obstacles and achieve your goals. As you apply resilience to different aspects of your life, you inspire others and create a supportive community.

Resilience isn't just about overcoming setbacks; it's about seeing challenges as opportunities for growth. By cultivating mental resilience through Krav Maga, you unlock your potential and create a life defined by strength, perseverance, and personal excellence.

CHAPTER 4

Confidence

"With each challenge faced in Krav Maga, the diamond of self-assurance emerges, transformed by pressure into an unbreakable spirit."

Dr. GM Neil Farber

In this chapter, we will delve into the significant mental advantage that Krav Maga brings - confidence! Confidence is an incredible quality that can have a profound influence on all areas of your life. We will explore how Krav Maga nurtures self-assuredness by honing your skills, instilling a belief in your capacity to navigate challenging situations, and boosting your self-esteem and self-belief.

Building Self-Assurance through Skill Development

Krav Maga builds confidence by teaching essential skills. During your training, you learn a wide range of practical self-defense techniques and strategies. With practice, you become skilled at executing these moves with precision and effectiveness. This not only improves your physical abilities but also boosts your self-assurance.

> *"In Krav Maga, confidence blooms like a lotus in a pond, nurtured by the waters of skill development and belief in one's capacity to handle any challenge."*

As you dedicate time and energy to mastering techniques, you'll see real improvements in your abilities. Developing your skills involves overcoming challenges, refining your movements, and surpassing your previous limits. Each little triumph reinforces your belief in your ability to learn and grow, leading to a sense of achievement that impacts all areas of your life.

When you gain confidence in your physical abilities, it spills over into your mental and emotional realms. Knowing that you can defend yourself effectively, you no longer feel vulnerable or helpless in the face of potential threats. This newfound self-assurance gives you a sense of security and empowerment, making it easier to navigate life with confidence.

Mastering Krav Maga techniques not only boosts your confidence, but also changes the way you view and handle challenging situations. It instills in you a sense of preparedness and resourcefulness, knowing that you have the tools to protect yourself and others if necessary. This heightened empowerment enables you to confront obstacles and adversity with a positive attitude, fully believing in your ability to handle whatever comes your way.

As you push yourself in Krav Maga, you gain resilience and determination that extend to all areas of your life. Overcoming challenges strengthens your mental fortitude, allowing you to face difficulties with confidence. Confidence is not just about showing off, it's about believing in yourself and your abilities. Krav Maga teaches you to trust your training and instincts, boosting your self-reliance and self-belief. This newfound confidence improves your mental well-being, relationships, and overall quality of life. Along your Krav Maga journey, you become a source of inspiration, encouraging others to find their own inner strength through Krav Maga.

Belief in Your Ability to Handle Difficult Situations

Krav Maga as a martial art that teaches practical self-defense for real-life situations, gives you the tools to analyze, assess, and respond effectively to dangerous situations. By training in realistic scenarios, you become familiar with high-stress situations and develop mental resilience. This builds your confidence and allows you to stay focused even in difficult circumstances. Each success reaffirms your belief in yourself and lays a strong foundation of confidence.

> *"In the realm of Krav Maga, confidence isn't just a fleeting emotion; it's a foundation, built brick by brick, shaping a fortress of self-belief."*

Krav Maga not only teaches you how to defend yourself physically, but it also has a profound impact on your mindset and self-belief. By pushing your limits and surpassing your own expectations, you tap into a well of inner strength and determination that you didn't know existed. This continuous process of growth and self-discovery builds your confidence, showing you that you can handle more challenges than you ever thought possible.

In addition, Krav Maga training prepares you for whatever life throws at you. You gain the tools and skills necessary to effectively confront and overcome any adversity. This newfound belief in your ability to handle difficult situations not only boosts your confidence, but also has a positive impact on your mental well-being. As your anxiety and fear decrease, you approach challenges with a sense of calm and composure. This allows you to make rational decisions and respond strategically, even when under pressure.

In Krav Maga training, you not only develop your physical abilities, but also experience a mental transformation that equips you to handle uncertainty and adapt to any situation with confidence. Through training, you learn to trust your instincts, make quick decisions without panicking, and overcome hesitation. This mental agility and belief in yourself empower you to take charge in difficult moments, boosting your overall self-assurance in every area of life.

As you progress in Krav Maga, you cultivate a deep belief in your own capabilities and resilience. This belief becomes an anchor that supports you through life's challenges, giving you the courage to face adversity head-on and the determination to pursue your goals. This newfound confidence extends beyond the training environment, becoming a source of inspiration for others as they witness your strength. Krav Maga transforms not only your ability to defend yourself physically, but also nurtures a sense of confidence and self-assurance that enables you to thrive in all aspects of life.

Enhancing Self-Esteem and Self-Efficacy

SThe relationship between self-esteem, self-efficacy, and confidence is strengthened through practicing Krav Maga. As you train and see improvement in your skills, your self-esteem is positively affected. Accomplishing challenging techniques or successfully defending yourself against opponents in training sessions gives you a sense of pride and self-worth. Setting and achieving goals in Krav Maga helps build self-efficacy, reinforcing your belief in your ability to succeed. The process of learning and mastering new techniques in Krav Maga demonstrates to yourself that you can acquire new skills through dedication and perseverance.

> *"Confidence thrives in the fertile soil of self-efficacy, and Krav Maga cultivates this belief, sowing seeds of assurance that bear fruits of courage."*

The supportive atmosphere of a Krav Maga class also boosts confidence, as you connect with others on a shared journey of self-improvement. This comprehensive approach to mental well-being enables you to face challenges with a positive mindset, knowing you can overcome them.

Confidence Applied

Krav Maga boosts your confidence, enhancing every part of your life and making you feel better overall. As you become mentally strong and self-assured by learning new skills and handling tough situations, you open the door to greater accomplishments and personal growth in many areas.

> *"As warriors in Krav Maga, we learn to stand tall, not only in combat but in life, fortified by the knowledge that we can navigate any storm."*

Let's explore how confidence, self-esteem, and self-efficacy help you thrive in different aspects of your life:

Personal Safety: Beyond the obvious benefits of self-defense, Krav Maga's mental training equips you with the confidence to navigate your surroundings with heightened situational awareness. This sense of security helps you to explore new places, engage in solo activities, and make decisions with a greater sense of independence.

Professional Life: The self-assurance gained from Krav Maga can positively impact your career. As you become more adept at overcoming challenges and adapting to dynamic situations, you approach professional tasks with a composed and solution-oriented mindset. This heightened confidence in your abilities can lead to increased productivity, better decision-making, and more significant contributions to your workplace.

Public Speaking: The mental fortitude and composure developed through Krav Maga training can translate to improved public speaking skills. The ability to face an audience with confidence and assertiveness allows you to deliver presentations more effectively and connect with others on a deeper level.

Social Interactions: The enhanced self-esteem and self-efficacy cultivated in Krav Maga class contribute to improved social interactions. Whether it's meeting new people, asserting boundaries, or handling conflicts, you approach social situations with greater self-assuredness, fostering healthier relationships and social connections.

Stress Management: Krav Maga's focus on resilience and mental toughness helps you cope with stress more effectively. The skill of remaining calm and composed under pressure in training, transfers to daily life, promoting overall well-being.

Goal Achievement: The belief in your ability to overcome obstacles gained through Krav Maga training becomes instrumental in pursuing personal goals. Whether it's fitness-related aspirations, academic pursuits, or personal projects, your confidence propels you forward and motivates you to persevere, increasing the likelihood of success.

Handling Life's Uncertainties: Life's unpredictability can sometimes be overwhelming. However, the resilience and adaptability developed in Krav Maga empower you to face uncertainties with a positive outlook and an agile approach. You learn to embrace change, confront challenges, and view setbacks as stepping stones to growth.

Leadership: Krav Maga training hones your leadership skills as you gain experience in guiding and supporting your fellow practitioners. This leadership mentality can extend to other areas of your life, like taking charge of group projects, and mentoring and inspiring others.

Positive Mindset: Confidence and self-assurance cultivate a positive mindset that influences your perspective on life. You develop a belief in your abilities, acknowledge your accomplishments, and cultivate self-compassion. This positive outlook fosters resilience and helps you find opportunities for growth even in challenging situations.

Emotional Regulation: Confidence acquired through Krav Maga training contributes to improved emotional regulation. As you become more self-assured, you better navigate emotions, responding to challenging situations with assertiveness rather than impulsively.

Conclusion

Confidence is a superpower that helps you face life's difficulties with strength and certainty. Krav Maga is more than just a physical discipline; it also shapes your mind and emotions. By learning new skills, believing in your ability to handle tough situations, and boosting your self-esteem and self-belief, Krav Maga becomes a life-changing tool for building confidence. And this newfound confidence spills over into every area of your life. Just remember, confidence takes time to develop, so be patient on your Krav Maga journey.

CHAPTER 5

Focus

"With every breath and every step, Krav Maga warriors harness the power of focus, transcending distractions to become masters of the moment."

Dr. GM Neil Farber

In the earlier chapters, we discovered how Krav Maga can improve your mental well-being by enhancing accountability, resilience and confidence. Now, let's dive into another vital topic: focus. Focus is a mental ability that plays a significant role in your training and everyday life. In this chapter, we'll explore how practicing Krav Maga can strengthen your focus and concentration, heighten your awareness of your surroundings, and enable you to make rapid decisions when faced with pressure.

Sharpening Your Focus and Concentration Skills

Krav Maga requires intense focus and concentration. When you train, you need to pay close attention to your instructor and training partners, learning their techniques and movements. Consistent practice helps you develop the ability to concentrate and sustain your attention for longer periods.

> *"Focus in Krav Maga is not just about narrowing vision; it's about sharpening the mind to stay present and aware, anticipating every move."*

The training drills in Krav Maga are complex and demanding. They require mental presence and focus. As you improve your skills, you become more in tune with your body, which enhances your coordination, reaction time, and overall efficiency. This heightened focus and concentration not only benefit your training but also spill over into other areas of your life, like work, school, and other physical activities.

In Krav Maga, you learn the importance of mindfulness and being fully present in the moment. This helps improve your awareness of your surroundings, emotions, and physical sensations. The ability to maintain focus during intense training also translates into better performance in academic or professional settings. You become better at concentrating on tasks without getting distracted, allowing you to excel and achieve better results.

Krav Maga places significant emphasis on situational awareness as a critical element of effective self-defense. Through Krav Maga training, you develop a heightened sense of awareness of your surroundings and potential threats. This enhanced awareness allows you to quickly assess and analyze situations, identifying potential dangers and making informed decisions on how to respond effectively.

Krav Maga focuses on being aware of your surroundings to effectively defend yourself. Training in Krav Maga helps you become more alert and vigilant, allowing you to assess threats and make quick decisions. You learn to anticipate and handle various scenarios, like multiple attackers or surprise attacks. By practicing these situations, you become better at processing information and responding appropriately. This improved situational awareness not only helps you deal with threats, but also enhances your overall sense of personal safety in everyday life..

Making Quick Decisions Under Pressure

In real-life self-defense situations, it is crucial to be able to think and act quickly. Krav Maga training helps you develop the skills to make swift decisions under pressure. By engaging in scenario-based simulations and dynamic sparring, you are exposed to high-stress situations that require immediate action.

> *"In the heart-pounding intensity of combat, focus illuminates the path, allowing us to navigate the darkness of uncertainty with resolute decisions."*

Practicing decision-making in these intense scenarios helps you become better at analyzing the situation, evaluating your options, and choosing the most appropriate response efficiently. This training helps you stay calm and focused, even in stressful and potentially dangerous situations. By training your mind to react decisively, you enhance your ability to effectively protect yourself and others in real-world encounters.

Krav Maga also teaches you the importance of adaptability and flexibility in decision- making. You learn to think on your feet and make necessary adjustments based on the evolving circumstances of a confrontation. This adaptability not only enhances your self- defense skills but also allows you to navigate other challenging situations in life with confidence and resilience.

The Focus Factor

Krav Maga training not only helps you defend yourself, but it also enhances your mental abilities. The skills you develop, like focus, concentration, and quick decision-making, have a broader application beyond just self-defense. These qualities can greatly influence different areas of your life, giving you the power to excel in any situation.

> *"The ability to tune out distractions and concentrate fully on the task at hand, instilled by Krav Maga, transforms everyday endeavors into opportunities for excellence."*

Let's take a closer look at the Focus Factor and how its positive impacts your life:

Academic and Professional Excellence: The skills learned in Krav Maga training can greatly benefit you in academic and professional settings. By learning to concentrate on complex tasks without getting distracted, you become better at absorbing and processing information. Whether you're studying for exams, working on assignments, or problem-solving, the enhanced focus from Krav Maga helps you be more efficient and perform better overall. With a clearer mind and improved attention management, you can excel academically and achieve professional success.

Enhanced Safety Awareness: The skills you learn in Krav Maga help you become more aware of your surroundings and the people around you in everyday life. This increased safety awareness allows you to confidently navigate busy streets, public spaces, and new places with a sense of vigilance. By recognizing and avoiding potential dangers, you can actively protect yourself and others, creating a safer environment for everyone.

Stress Management and Decision Making: The art of making smart choices in tough situations is a precious skill learned in Krav Maga. It helps you handle stress and conquer obstacles. When faced with difficulties, you can rely on your training to stay cool and collected. This allows you to think clearly, consider different paths, and respond wisely. With this mental strength, you can tackle stressful circumstances with confidence and make better decisions in all areas of life.

Effective Conflict Resolution: Krav Maga teaches you to be adaptable and flexible in making decisions, which helps you resolve conflicts better. By learning to think quickly and adapt to changing situations, you become better at dealing with disagreements between people. You learn when to stand up for yourself, when to find middle ground, and when to step away from tense situations. Being able to communicate confidently and handle conflicts in a positive way improves your relationships, both in your personal life and at work.

Increased Self-Confidence and Self-Efficacy: When you practice Krav Maga, your ability to concentrate, stay aware of your surroundings, and make decisions quickly improves.

This boosts your confidence as you face challenges and push yourself to new limits. This newfound belief in yourself extends beyond your martial arts training and spills over into every area of your life. You become more assertive in making choices and more open to seizing opportunities. With your increased self-belief, you feel empowered to tackle new challenges head-on, knowing that you have the necessary skills and mental strength to triumph.

Conclusion

Krav Maga training has a powerful effect on your focus, making a positive impact on all areas of your life. It helps you sharpen your focus, become more aware of your surroundings, and make quick decisions. This not only helps you excel academically and professionally, but also boosts your safety awareness and helps you manage stress effectively. These mental skills also come in handy for resolving conflicts, boosting self-confidence, and promoting personal growth through mindfulness. Being focused not only improves your self-defense abilities, but also makes you a confident, resilient, and empowered individual in all aspects of life. To enhance your focus further, commit to regular practice and stay fully present during your training sessions. Embrace challenges and strive to push beyond your limits. This will not only enhance your Krav Maga skills, but also have a positive impact on your focus and mental sharpness in every area of your life.

CHAPTER 6

Stress Relief

"The cathartic release of stress through Krav Maga unleashes a sense of clarity and peace, reminding us that we are capable of overcoming any mental or physical obstacle."

Dr. GM Neil Farber

In this chapter I will discuss the importance of managing stress for our mental health. Stress can have negative effects on both our mind and body, and modern life tends to be very demanding. However, I will show how practicing Krav Maga can be an effective tool for relieving stress. Through Krav Maga training, we can not only manage our stress levels but also use it as a healthy outlet for our emotions. Ultimately, incorporating Krav Maga into our lives can contribute to our overall mental well-being.

Krav Maga as a Powerful Stress Management Tool

Krav Maga is a great way to manage and release stress. The intense workouts and self-defense techniques help you channel built-up tension and redirect your focus away from stressors. This promotes a sense of calm and clarity. Krav Maga also provides a structured environment where you can take a break from everyday challenges and solely focus on training. This mental respite allows your mind to recharge and rejuvenate.

> *"Krav Maga instills a warrior's calm in the face of adversity, proving that stress management is not about avoiding pressure but embracing it with courage."*

Physical activity, such as Krav Maga training, is well-known for its ability to release endorphins and promote a positive mood. Engaging in regular physical exercise stimulates the production of endorphins, which are natural chemicals in the body that help reduce stress and elevate mood. As a result, Krav Maga training can serve as an effective stress management tool, promoting overall mental well-being.Physical activity, such as Krav Maga training, is well-known for its ability to release endorphins and promote a positive mood. Engaging in regular physical exercise stimulates the production of endorphins, which are natural chemicals in the body that help reduce stress and elevate mood. As a result, Krav Maga training can serve as an effective stress management tool, promoting overall mental well-being.

The physicality of Krav Maga, with its dynamic movements and intense workouts, allows you to release physical tension and built-up stress. The combination of cardio exercises, strength training, and self-defense techniques not only improves your physical fitness but you will also

experience a release of muscular tension and promotes relaxation.

Channeling Emotions in a Positive Way

Emotions are powerful influencers in our lives and can sometimes lead to stress. But there's a beneficial way to handle them: Krav Maga training. This training provides a positive outlet for your emotions. It encourages you to recognize and embrace your feelings, using them to empower your movements and skills. Instead of letting frustration, anger, or fear consume you, you can redirect them in a controlled way through your training, transforming them into productive energy and finding release.

Krav Maga training helps you control your emotions. It teaches self-discipline and helps you stay calm and focused, even in tough situations. This skill is useful not just during training, but also in your daily life. It helps you handle stress better and remain strong and composed.

Additionally, practicing Krav Maga promotes a feeling of success and inner strength. As you learn and excel in new skills, your confidence grows, enhancing your overall self-worth and mental health. This newfound belief in yourself extends to your everyday experiences, helping you to face obstacles with a more optimistic and resilient attitude.

De-Stress not Distress

Krav Maga goes beyond just relieving stress through intense workouts. It also helps improve mental health and overall well-being. By learning stress relief techniques in Krav Maga, practitioners can apply them to different areas of life, leading to a stronger mindset and emotional resilience.

> *"Krav Maga's emphasis on practical self-defense empowers individuals physically and mentally, instilling a sense of self-assurance that reduces stress in everyday situations."*

Here are a few examples of how Krav Maga stress relief can positively influence your life:

Mindful Stress Management: Krav Maga teaches the value of staying focused and present during training, which also helps in everyday life to handle stress better. Through practicing mindfulness, you can recognize what causes stress and use techniques to manage it before it becomes overwhelming.

Improved Coping Strategies: Krav Maga training empowers you to conquer challenges in a calm and effective way. It teaches valuable skills for managing stress and provides tools to handle the pressures of both personal and professional life. Instead of feeling overwhelmed, you become more skilled at facing stressors directly and dealing with them calmly.

Embracing Resilience: Resilience is crucial for reducing stress, and Krav Maga goes beyond physical training to develop mental toughness. By learning how to recover from setbacks and embrace adversity as a chance to grow, you develop a mindset that sees stress as challenges to conquer instead of overwhelming hurdles.

Emotional Release and Regulation: Krav Maga allows you to safely express your emotions and use them in your movements. This helps reduce emotional tension and brings a sense of release. Additionally, the practice teaches how to regulate emotions, so you can respond calmly to stress.

Boosting Self-Esteem and Self-Confidence: As you advance in your Krav Maga training, you experience a sense of achievement and self-assurance. This boost in confidence spills over into your everyday life, giving you the courage to face obstacles with optimism and a strong belief in yourself.

Social Support and Community: Krav Maga training is about unity and teamwork. When you train, your fellow practitioners become more than just training partners - they become your friends and biggest supporters. This tight-knit community provides a strong support system that extends beyond the gym. Not only does this support system help you navigate difficult times, but it also has a positive impact on your mental well-being.

Mind-Body Connection: Krav Maga training focuses on uniting the mind and body. Through this practice, you develop a heightened awareness of your physical sensations and mental condition, thus strengthening your mind-body connection. By being more in tune with yourself, you can effectively identify signs of stress and take necessary steps to prevent them from escalating.

Conclusion

Krav Krav Maga is a great stress reliever. It helps you release tension, control your emotions, and improve your mental well-being. When you do intense physical training, you can shift your attention away from stressful things and feel more calm and clear-headed. By channeling your emotions in a positive way, you can turn them into productive energy. Plus, the endorphins released during training make you feel good and improve your overall mental health.

The structured nature of Krav Maga training gives you a break from the pressures of everyday life. It's a chance for your mind to rest and recharge. By doing Krav Maga regularly, you can proactively manage and reduce the impact of stress on your mental and physical health.

CHAPTER 7

Discipline And Self-Control

"Krav Maga teaches not just physical discipline, but the mental tenacity to push past limits and achieve greatness."

Dr. GM Neil Farber

In earlier chapters, we discovered how Krav Maga enhances our mental well-being with benefits like resilience, confidence, focus, and stress relief. Now, let's explore another vital aspect: discipline and self-control. Krav Maga not only sharpens our physical abilities but also nurtures our mental discipline and self-control. In this chapter, we will examine how Krav Maga fosters discipline and self-control, empowers us to handle emotions and make logical choices, and how these mental strengths can positively impact other aspects of our lives. There exists some variations in Krav Maga techniques and strategies between various organizations. However, one principle that all respected instructors emphasize is discipline. Whether you're reading books by renowned authors like Eyal

Yanilov, Darren Levine, John Whitman, David Kahn, Gerson Ben Keren, or Tommi Nystrom, or engaging in discussions with experts like Dr. Itay Gil, Nir Maman, Moshe Galisko, or Moti Horenstein, the importance of discipline in training is always highlighted. It is a fundamental aspect integrated into Krav Maga training at every level.

Cultivating Discipline through Training

Krav Maga training demands discipline and self-control. From the moment you step onto the training mat, you are expected to follow instructions, adhere to the techniques and principles, and maintain focus throughout the session. The structured nature of Krav Maga, with its defined techniques and progressive curriculum, helps instill discipline and self-control into your practice.

To cultivate discipline and self-control in Krav Maga, you are constantly challenged in various aspects of training. One way is by sticking to the training schedule. Regular attendance and being on time are crucial in Krav Maga as they show your dedication to the practice. You learn to prioritize training sessions and fit them into your daily routine, even when faced with other responsibilities or distractions. By consistently attending training and pushing yourself to improve, you develop the mental strength and self-discipline needed to excel in Krav Maga and other areas of life.

> *"Krav Maga's emphasis on discipline empowers individuals to face adversity head-on, equipping them with the tools to conquer fears and embrace personal growth."*

Suppose you're a busy person with a tiring job. But despite feeling exhausted, you make a point of regularly attending your Krav Maga class. This commitment helps you develop the discipline to push through fatigue and stay focused during training. And that discipline translates into your professional life, helping you handle challenging situations.

Krav Maga also emphasizes precise and controlled movements. Learning to execute each technique with accuracy teaches you self-control. This self-control not only improves the effectiveness of your movements but also reduces the risk of injuries. In turn, this promotes a safe training environment.

In a self-defense situation, having self-control is crucial. It means that you will respond to an aggressor with just enough force to stop the threat, without going overboard. This helps to prevent the situation from getting worse and allows for a more controlled ending.

Another important aspect of Krav Maga training is setting clear goals. As you advance in your training and strive to master different techniques, you start to understand the importance of discipline in reaching these goals. This process of setting and working towards goals helps you stay focused and committed, leading to a strong work ethic that goes beyond just training.

Krav Maga training takes you to the limits of your physical and mental abilities. When faced with tough techniques or difficult situations, discipline becomes crucial to overcome obstacles and keep progressing. By setting goals and working hard to achieve them, you develop self-control, which helps you conquer challenges and reach higher levels of skill.

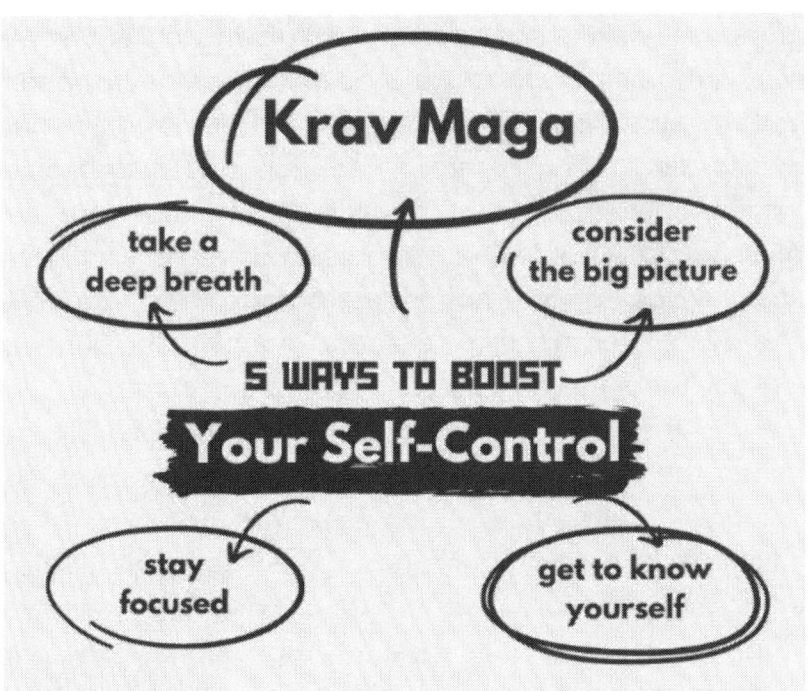

The guidance of instructors and support from training partners also reinforces the importance of discipline and self-control in Krav Maga. Instructors stress the value of consistent practice, dedication, and respecting others during training. Your training partners work together and motivate each other, fostering a culture of discipline and camaraderie within the Krav Maga community.

Managing Emotions and Making Rational Decisions

Krav Maga training is intense, putting you in challenging situations that can make you feel scared, frustrated, or angry. But, it also teaches you how to control your emotions and make smart decisions. One of the core principles of Krav Maga is staying calm in high-pressure moments. By learning to manage your emotions, you're able to think clearly and react effectively. During training, you're taught to override impulsive responses and instead, respond with careful thought. Through repetitive drills and realistic simulations, you develop the ability to analyze situations objectively. You're able to assess potential threats, consider your options, and choose the best response based on logic, rather than just emotions. This skill is incredibly valuable in real-life scenarios, where making quick and effective decisions can be life-saving.

> *"In Krav Maga, rational decision-making becomes second nature, as practitioners learn to trust their instincts and leverage their training to respond effectively to any situation."*

Krav Maga training can be intense and emotional. One of the most challenging parts is defending against simulated attacks. In these drills, you'll face an aggressive opponent, and it's natural to feel fear and adrenaline. But, with practice, you can learn how to control your fight or flight response. This allows you to think clearly and react effectively.

For example, when you first start Krav Maga, facing an attacker may be terrifying. However, as you continue training, you'll learn to manage these emotions. Instead of panicking, you'll focus on using self-defense techniques. This emotional control not only improves your performance in class but also helps keep you safe in real-life situations.

Krav Maga teaches you how to handle real-life situations by practicing scenarios that mimic actual encounters. These scenarios help you make quick decisions and think clearly, even when you're feeling stressed. For instance, imagine being faced with multiple attackers – you learn to analyze the situation, identify threats, and determine the best action to take. This kind of training builds your mental discipline, enabling you to stay calm and focused in high-pressure situations. These skills are not only useful on the training mat but also in your everyday life, helping you handle difficult situations with confidence and composure.

Translating Mental Discipline into Other Areas

The mental discipline and self-control cultivated through Krav Maga training have far-reaching benefits beyond the training mat. The ability to manage your emotions and make rational decisions carries over into various aspects of your life, including personal relationships, work, and other endeavors.

In personal relationships, discipline and self-control allow you to communicate effectively, listen attentively, and respond thoughtfully rather than react impulsively. You become more aware of your emotions and can navigate conflicts with composure and empathy, fostering healthier and more constructive interactions.

In the professional world, discipline plays a vital role in helping you stay on track, reach your goals, and work hard towards them. It helps you handle stress, resist distractions, and make thoughtful choices, ultimately boosting your productivity and success in your chosen career.

But discipline isn't just limited to work. By applying the same principles to other aspects of your life like personal growth, education, decision-making, hobbies, and personal goals, you can make remarkable progress and experience significant growth. So, embrace discipline and commitment in all areas of your life, and watch yourself thrive.

Academic Pursuits: Practicing Krav Maga teaches you to set clear goals and maintain focus, which can be transferred to your studies. By creating a study schedule and sticking to it, you become more effective and efficient in your academic endeavors. Additionally, the ability to stay calm and handle stress during exams enables you to think clearly and perform at your highest level even under pressure.

Healthy Habits: Krav Maga promotes a holistic approach to health and wellness, and this discipline extends to other aspects of your well-being, including nutrition and exercise. Through the commitment and self-control developed in training, you can adopt and maintain healthy habits in your daily life. Whether it's maintaining a balanced diet, getting regular exercise, or getting enough rest, the mental discipline from Krav Maga empowers you to prioritize your health and well-being.

In Krav Maga, your self-control can help you make healthier food choices when tempted by unhealthy options. This promotes both your physical and mental well-being. Moreover, the commitment to regular exercise in Krav Maga can motivate you to establish consistent workout routines, resulting in improved overall fitness and a better state of being.

Personal Growth and Resilience: In the practice of Krav Maga, the mental strength and determination you develop can have a profound impact on your personal development. This martial art teaches you how to overcome obstacles and setbacks, both in training and in life. By staying committed to your goals and persevering through challenges, you can achieve remarkable growth and resilience.

The principles of discipline and self-control that you learn in Krav Maga can be applied to all aspects of your life. Whether you are pursuing hobbies or striving for personal growth, having the ability to stay focused and push through difficulties is essential. Just like how you work to improve your techniques in Krav Maga, you can apply the same level of dedication and perseverance to overcome obstacles and continue progressing in other areas of your life. Don't underestimate the power of the mental discipline developed through Krav Maga. It is a valuable tool that can enable you to achieve your desired outcomes and become a stronger, more resilient individual.

Decision-making and Problem-solving: Krav Maga training improves your ability to think and act quickly and logically, even in stressful situations. This skill can be applied to everyday problem-solving. You become better at understanding complicated situations, finding possible solutions, and making wise decisions.

For example, at work, when dealing with a difficult project or an important choice, the discipline and self-control you learn in Krav Maga help you stay composed, think carefully, and overcome obstacles with clarity and focus. This can result in more successful problem-solving and decision-making, ultimately benefiting your career.

By incorporating these skills into personal relationships, work, academics, health habits, personal growth, and decision-making, you can become a more composed, productive, and resilient individual. Krav Maga is not just about physical self-defense; it has the power to transform you into a well-rounded person capable of confidently overcoming life's obstacles with determination and focus.

By mastering the art of emotional regulation and rational decision-making through training, you will develop valuable life skills that can be applied to everyday challenges. Whether it's handling conflicts with composure, making thoughtful choices, or nurturing healthy relationships, these skills will empower you to navigate life successfully.

Conclusion

Krav Maga training teaches discipline and self-control. By practicing regularly and following the principles of Krav Maga, you build the mental strength to stay focused, overcome challenges, and make rational decisions. This discipline doesn't just stay on the training mat—it spreads to other areas of your life.

By managing your emotions and making thoughtful choices, you can handle conflicts, manage stress, and stay composed in high-pressure situations. Being able to control your emotional reactions helps you communicate effectively, form stronger relationships, and approach obstacles with a calm and clear mindset.

The mental discipline and self-control you gain from Krav Maga training also have a positive impact on other parts of your life. Whether it's in school, work, personal goals, or everyday tasks, the discipline you develop in Krav Maga can help you stay focused, be more productive, and achieve success.

By incorporating discipline and self-control into your daily routine, you can better achieve your goals, conquer obstacles, and maintain a positive outlook. Krav Maga, a form of self-defense, helps develop these qualities by teaching you how to manage your emotions and make rational decisions. This goes beyond just protecting yourself

- it equips you with life skills that foster focus, resilience, and discipline. By embracing the mental aspects of Krav Maga, you can experience personal growth, success, and overall well-being in all areas of your life. In the next chapter, we will explore how practicing mindfulness in Krav Maga can enhance your training and bring about mental and emotional benefits, helping you find inner peace and harmony.

CHAPTER 8

Mindfulness

"The greatest warriors know that mastering the self through mindfulness is the first step to mastering Krav Maga."

Dr. GM Neil Farber

In this chapter we're going to focus on mindfulness in Krav Maga. Mindfulness means being fully present in the moment and being aware of your thoughts, emotions, and physical sensations. To truly benefit from all the mental and physical advantages of Krav Maga, you need to practice mindfulness. In this chapter, we'll see how Krav Maga incorporates and promotes mindfulness, the advantages of being present during training, and how Krav Maga can improve your overall well-being as a mindful movement practice.

Practicing Present-Moment Awareness in Training

In Krav Maga, the intense and dynamic training environment provides a unique opportunity to practice present-moment awareness. Many top instructors, such as David Kahn, Darren Levine, John Whitman, and Eyal Yanilov, emphasize mindfulness and awareness alongside physical techniques. Whether you are defending yourself, participating in partner drills, or simulating real-life situations, being fully focused and present is crucial. Split-second decisions can mean the difference between success and failure in self-defense scenarios, especially in Krav Maga.

By sharpening your concentration skills and immersing yourself in the training, you improve your ability to respond effectively and efficiently to any situation that arises.

> *"In the heart of Krav Maga lies the power of the present; for in truly seeing, sensing, and acting in the now, we find our truest defense and strength."*

During Krav Maga training, distractions fade away and you become fully attuned to the immediate task at hand. This leads to enhanced physical performance and heightened awareness of your surroundings. With this heightened focus, you can better understand and collaborate with your training partners, picking up on subtle cues during drills. Additionally, Krav Maga teaches you to block out distractions and focus solely on the task at hand, whether it's executing a technique, assessing a threat, or responding to an attack. Being fully present during each training session allows you to absorb and internalize the knowledge and skills being taught, resulting in continuous improvement in your techniques and overall proficiency.

Remaining mentally present during Krav Maga training is extremely important for being adaptable. As the situations change, being fully engaged allows you to adjust and respond appropriately. Practicing present-moment awareness consistently sharpens your ability to handle unpredictable self-defense scenarios.

By fully immersing yourself in the present moment during Krav Maga training, you develop a stronger mind-body connection. This heightened awareness of your physical actions, breathing, and mental focus helps you improve your movements, balance, and power in techniques. The mindfulness cultivated through present-moment awareness in Krav Maga is a valuable skill that enhances your performance in training.

Using Krav Maga as Mindful Movement Practice

Krav Maga itself can be seen as a mindful movement practice, as it requires full engagement of your body and mind. Each technique and movement is executed with intention, precision, and focus, fostering a deep connection between your physical actions and your mental state. It encompasses how you approach every aspect of training.

> *"Every step, every strike in Krav Maga is a meditation; it's the mindful movement that transforms the practitioner from reactive to proactive, from fearful to fearless."*

Now let's explore some specific examples of how Krav Maga can be beneficial as a mindful movement practice:

Intention and Precision: In Krav Maga, every move is thoughtful and driven by purpose. Whether it's a strike, block, or dodge, every technique is approached with clear intent. Take punching for example, it's not just about hitting the target, but also about generating power from your core and keeping your body properly aligned. This deliberate and precise approach results in more successful and powerful techniques.

Focused Breathing: In Krav Maga, being aware of your movement is made even more effective when combined with mindful breathing. Throughout your training, you are taught to match your breath with your actions. For instance, exhaling as you strike not only helps to relieve stress but also increases the power behind your movements. By focusing on your breath, your mind becomes more peaceful and you are better able to stay in control even in high-pressure situations.

Body Awareness: As you progress in Krav Maga, you develop a heightened sense of body awareness. Developing a keen sense of your body's balance, weight distribution, and muscle engagement helps you identify weaknesses in your stance or defense. By being self-aware, you can make adjustments that enhance your stability and make you more effective.

Flow State: Flow is a state of total focus and complete involvement in an activity. In Krav Maga, doing repetitive drills and techniques can help you achieve this state of flow. When you smoothly move through the motions, distractions disappear, and you become fully present in the moment. This calm and focused mindset in Krav Maga not only improves your performance but also gives you clarity.

Adaptability and Responsiveness: Mindful movement fosters adaptability in Krav Maga. When you're fully focused during training, you can better understand and react to your partner's movements and intentions. For example, when doing partner drills, you become skilled at recognizing their attack patterns and adjusting your defense accordingly. This improved responsiveness helps you react quickly and effectively in real-life situations.

Mind-Body Connection: In Krav Maga, mindful movement deepens the connection between your physical actions and mental focus. This means being aware of how your body is aligned, your breathing, your balance, your energy, and your intention as you throw punches or kicks. By paying attention to these details, you can make your techniques more effective and improve your coordination. When you consciously engage your muscles and coordinate your movements, you become more in tune with your body and gain a better understanding of what it can do.

Stress Relief: Krav Maga's mindful movement practice is a great way to relieve stress and let go of emotional burdens. During training, you can effectively channel your frustrations and tensions through powerful strikes and controlled movements. This not only helps you manage stress but also leaves you feeling calm and empowered.

By immersing yourself in this mindful movement practice, you gain a deeper understanding of yourself and enhance your self-defense capabilities. The intentional approach, focused breathing, body awareness, flow state, adaptability, mind-body connection, and stress-relief aspects of Krav Maga make it a holistic and effective form of self-defense training.

Cultivating Mindfulness to Enhance Well-being

Mindfulness in Krav Maga goes beyond the training mat and benefits your everyday life. It improves your well-being by making you more self-aware, helping you control your emotions, and clearing your mind.

> *"Krav Maga's teachings of mindfulness ripple outwards, offering a compass for navigating the intricate dance of daily life with grace and resilience."*

Practicing mindfulness allows you to be more in tune with your thoughts, feelings, and physical sensations. This allows you to respond calmly instead of reacting impulsively when faced with challenging situations. By observing your internal experiences without judgment, you can better manage stress, anxiety, and other negative emotions that may arise during training or in your daily life. With mindfulness, you develop inner calm and resilience, which helps you stay focused when dealing with adversity. As a result, you are better equipped to handle difficult situations with clarity and composure. By adopting a non-reactive mindset, you gain more control over your responses and become less affected by external circumstances.

Cultivating mindfulness through Krav Maga has numerous benefits that extend to everyday life, here are some examples of how mindfulness is beneficial in daily life:

Emotional Regulation: Practicing mindfulness helps us better understand our feelings and accept them without any judgment. This awareness of our emotions allows us to respond to them in a positive way, rather than acting on impulse. Research demonstrates that mindfulness-based interventions can greatly improve emotional regulation and lessen symptoms of anxiety and depression.

Positivity and Optimism: Mindfulness practices enhance positive emotions and cultivate a brighter perspective on life. By training oneself to concentrate on the present and release thoughts about the past or concerns about the future, people can discover a newfound sense of happiness, appreciation, and fulfillment.

Improved Immunity: Mindfulness practice is linked to improved immune system functioning. Regular practice can boost the body's ability to fight off illnesses, leading to better overall health and increased resistance to sickness.

Brain Health and Aging: Studies have found that mindfulness meditation can benefit brain health. People who regularly practice mindfulness have shown to have less shrinkage in certain brain areas that tend to decrease with age. This indicates that mindfulness might assist in maintaining brain health and cognitive function as we grow older.

Resilience and Coping Skills: Mindfulness practice helps us become more resilient by being able to adapt and recover from tough situations. By staying focused and calm during stressful times, we can navigate challenges more effectively. This leads to better coping skills and mental strength.

Increased Life Satisfaction: Practicing mindfulness is the key to finding true happiness and fulfillment. When we fully engage with the present moment, we can fully experience the joys of life and develop a stronger appreciation for what we already have.

Numerous research studies have consistently shown that practicing mindfulness has a positive impact on both mental and physical well-being. This means that engaging in mindfulness activities can reduce stress, anxiety, symptoms of depression, and generally improve overall psychological health and quality of life. There are many great books on the benefits of mindfulness in health & wellness. Two authors I highly recommend are *Ellen Langer* and *Jon Kabat-Zinn*. While there approaches are very different, they are both highly relevant. I would start with Langer's, *"The Mindful Body: Thinking Our Way to Chronic Health"* and Kabat-Zinn's *"Full Catastrophe Living: Using the Wisdom of Your Body and Mind to Face Stress, Pain, and Illness"*. Then read everything else that they've written!

Now, by incorporating the mindful movement practice of Krav Maga into your daily routine, you can go beyond reaping the benefits only during training sessions. By being more aware, intentional, and focused on the present moment in your everyday activities, you can establish a deeper connection with yourself and the world around you. The moving meditation aspect of Krav Maga also offers a valuable tool to relieve stress, which can be used during difficult moments, enhancing your mental well-being and emotional resilience in your day-to-day life.

Ultimately, developing mindfulness through Krav Maga empowers you to lead a more balanced, purposeful, and fulfilling life.

Conclusion

Mindfulness is a powerful practice that can improve your well-being and should be part of Krav Maga. When you practice being aware of the present moment during training, you become more focused, concentrated, and better at making decisions. And when you practice mindfulness outside of training, it helps you handle stress, control your emotions, and deal with difficult situations more calmly and clearly.

Krav Maga itself is a mindful practice, where every technique and movement is done with intention and precision. By moving mindfully, you connect your mind and body, become more aware of your body's movements, and improve your overall physical performance. Krav Maga can also be a form of meditation in motion, helping you enter a state of flow, relieve stress, and find inner calm.

When you incorporate mindfulness into your Krav Maga practice, you benefit in many areas of your life. Being fully present and focused carries over to your everyday activities, making you more productive, focused, and effective. Mindfulness also cultivates a deeper understanding of yourself, better control of your emotions, and the ability to adapt and handle challenges with poise and resilience.

CHAPTER 9

Communication

"Krav Maga teaches us that true communication isn't just about speaking louder, but listening deeper; sensing intent, understanding movement, and responding with purpose."

Dr. GM Neil Farber

Communication is essential in Krav Maga, beyond just the physical moves. It is vital for self-defense, teamwork, and forming connections within the Krav Maga community. In this chapter, we will delve into why communication matters in Krav Maga, how training improves communication skills, and how assertiveness, body language, and effective self-expression help resolve conflicts and foster better relationships.

Enhancing Communication Skills through Training

In Krav Maga training, effective communication is a vital component that ensures the safety and success of both the attacker and the defender. Clear and precise communication is essential during techniques and drills in a dynamic and challenging environment, allowing individuals to convey their intentions effectively and coordinate movements seamlessly with their training partners.

> *"Krav Maga doesn't just sharpen the body; it fine-tunes the art of listening, teaching us that the most profound dialogues are those where actions and intentions align in harmony."*

In Krav Maga training, effective communication is crucial for the safety and success of both the attacker and the defender. By clearly conveying intentions and coordinating movements, individuals can prevent accidents, injuries, and ensure smooth execution of techniques.

When practicing joint locks or grappling techniques, verbal cues are essential to execute moves smoothly and prevent mishaps. By consistently developing communication skills during training, individuals become proficient at expressing intentions clearly, allowing their partners to respond appropriately and perform techniques accurately.

In partner drills and simulations, communication becomes even more critical. Clear and concise commands enable seamless coordination between training partners. During scenarios with multiple attackers, assertive communication is necessary for the defender to effectively manage the situation. By setting boundaries and signaling readiness to engage or disengage, individuals maintain a safe training environment and navigate the scenario with precision.

Therefore, clear and effective communication is a vital component in Krav Maga training, facilitating coordination, safety, and successful execution of techniques.

In Krav Maga training, paying attention to what others say and how they move is really important. It helps you predict what they might do and react quickly. This makes you more aware of your surroundings during training so you can react fast to unexpected situations.

Communication is especially important when practicing techniques with weapons. Whether it's fake guns, knives, or other improvised weapons, clear and concise communication is crucial for keeping everyone safe.

When dealing with weapons, there is a lot at stake, and any misunderstanding can be dangerous. Talking and giving clear instructions become very important during weapon drills. For example, when practicing how to take a weapon away from someone, the defender needs to let their training partner know that they are ready and explain exactly what they plan to do. This helps the partner adjust their grip or position to make the training safe and controlled.

Krav Maga emphasizes the importance of actively listening in various scenarios, including those involving weapons. When training with partners who are using weapons, it is crucial to pay close attention to their commands and cues in order to ensure a proper response. Active listening helps in accurately interpreting and following instructions, reducing the risk of misunderstandings and creating a safer training environment.

In addition to physical techniques, Krav Maga training also focuses on developing essential verbal communication skills for real-life self-defense situations. One key skill is verbal de-escalation, which involves using calm and assertive language to defuse potentially volatile situations and avoid physical confrontations. By effectively communicating with potential attackers or aggressors, the intensity of the conflict can be lowered, preventing escalation and providing opportunities for safe disengagement.

Krav Maga training teaches you how to use verbal skills to manipulate the environment and position yourself advantageously. For example, when facing a gun threat from behind, you might communicate persuasively with the attacker while you slowly turn around to perform a gun defense technique from the front instead. By employing strategic communication, you can manipulate the situation, create a more advantageous position, and increase the chances of successful self-defense.

By integrating verbal de-escalation, distraction, and manipulation techniques into Krav Maga training, you gain the ability to defuse conflicts, create opportunities for escape or counterattack, and position yourself advantageously to enhance your safety and self-defense effectiveness in real-world situations.

In Krav Maga training, good communication is important for safety and trust with your partners. When dealing with weapons, trust is crucial as you rely on your partners to handle them properly. Effective communication also promotes teamwork and cooperation, leading to better training sessions. By practicing clear and concise communication in Krav Maga, you become more aware of your surroundings and can handle dangerous situations calmly. These communication skills also apply to real-life self-defense situations, where effective communication can make a difference in the outcome. Overall, improving communication in Krav Maga is vital for safety and success in self-defense.

Assertiveness, Non-Verbal Cues, and Effective Self-Expression

In Krav Maga, being assertive is more than just using words - it involves using non-verbal cues as well. These cues are crucial for effective self-defense and communication. By paying attention to an aggressor's body language, facial expressions, and posture, you can determine how aggressive they are and whether they intend to attack or harm someone. This information allows you to respond appropriately, either by taking action to defend yourself or by trying to calm the situation down.

Non-verbal cues can also be used strategically to distract an attacker and create opportunities for defense or escape. For example, you might gesture towards your wallet, diverting the attacker's attention while positioning yourself for a counterattack or escape. By using non-verbal signals effectively, you can disrupt an attacker's focus, gain a temporary advantage, and find ways to defend yourself.

> *"Through Krav Maga we discover that effective communication is about cultivating an attuned sense of receptivity, where every gesture speaks volumes."*

Having strong non-verbal communication skills is crucial in partner drills and training scenarios. This involves using assertive body language and cues to convey intentions and coordinate movements effectively. When you project confidence and assertiveness through your body language, you improve your ability to lead and direct the interaction during training, leading to better collaboration and learning outcomes.

In self-defense situations, having poor non-verbal communication skills can have serious consequences, even life-threatening ones. It is crucial to be able to interpret the intentions and cues of an aggressor accurately, as well as use non-verbal cues as distractions. These skills are essential to develop for self-defense.

Additionally, Krav Maga training focuses on effective self-expression. This enables you to assertively and constructively articulate your thoughts, concerns, and emotions. By learning to express yourself clearly and confidently, you can establish boundaries and effectively communicate your needs during training and in other aspects of life. This ability to assertively express oneself contributes to a positive training environment and promotes effective communication with training partners and instructors.

Mastering assertiveness in Krav Maga means learning to communicate confidently and respectfully, without being aggressive. It's important to differentiate between assertive language and tone, which is firm and self-assured, and aggressive communication, which is confrontational and hostile. By training in Krav Maga, you develop the ability to express yourself assertively, without resorting to aggression. This allows you to remain composed and poised in challenging situations. By combining assertiveness with non-verbal cues and effective self-expression, you improve your overall communication skills. You become better at identifying potential threats, setting boundaries, and confidently handling real-life situations.

Conflict Resolution and Interpersonal Dynamics

Krav Maga emphasizes the importance of conflict resolution and fostering positive interpersonal dynamics. You learn how to defuse tense situations and find non-violent solutions. Effective and assertive communication helps to prevent aggression and redirect interactions. Empathy and respect are also fostered towards training partners and fellow practitioners, creating a supportive training environment of open communication and active listening.

Communication is important not only in partner drills but also in everyday interactions. By honing communication skills, practitioners become more assertive, improve non-verbal cues, and express themselves effectively. It helps you develop a deeper understanding of others' perspectives and needs.

By communicating intentions, coordinating movements, and providing feedback, individuals can work together seamlessly, maximizing the effectiveness of their training and achieving shared goals. This all contributes to a cohesive and supportive Krav Maga community.

Communication is Key

Effective communication is essential in our daily lives, impacting our relationships, work, family dynamics, and business interactions. While verbal communication is important, non-verbal communication actually makes up about 70% of overall communication. Krav Maga training teaches valuable lessons that apply to all areas of life, improving our ability to communicate with confidence and assertiveness.

One key aspect of communication that Krav Maga training enhances is self-expression. Through training, you learn to express your thoughts, concerns, and emotions in a positive and assertive way. This skill allows you to effectively communicate in various situations, such as giving feedback, resolving conflicts, and expressing your needs and desires. Effective self-expression fosters understanding, strengthens relationships, and creates a more harmonious and productive environment.

For instance, as a teacher or boss, you can provide constructive feedback to students or employees, clearly expressing expectations and areas for improvement while maintaining a respectful and supportive tone.

Enhancing communication skills in Krav Maga has profound benefits for conflict resolution and interpersonal dynamics. Through practicing effective communication techniques, you are able to de-escalate conflicts,  actively listen to others, and seek non-violent resolutions. Being able to communicate assertively and respectfully during conflicts empowers you to diffuse tension, find common ground, and maintain positive relationships. This becomes particularly valuable in romantic relationships, where effective communication allows for conveying needs and boundaries, fostering understanding and mutual respect.

Krav Maga training also places a strong emphasis on teamwork and cooperation. This creates a culture that values open communication and mutual respect. By effectively communicating intentions, coordinating movements, and providing constructive feedback, individuals are able to create a supportive and collaborative training environment. These communication skills not only foster camaraderie and trust, but also contribute to mutual growth in all relationships.

> *"In Krav Maga, every movement speaks a language; when we communicate with precision, clarity, and respect, we transcend mere combat, elevating it to a dialogue of souls."*

In In Krav Maga, non-verbal communication plays a crucial role. Body language, facial expressions, and posture can send powerful messages that can influence the outcome of a situation. By mastering these non-verbal cues, individuals can project confidence, discourage potential threats, and effectively convey their intentions. This heightened awareness of non-verbal communication goes beyond self-defense scenarios and can have a positive impact on interpersonal interactions in daily life. For example, in a business setting, you can use confident body language and active listening to make a successful business deal and establish a strong professional connection.

Additionally, being attuned to subtle non-verbal cues can help tailor your sales pitch to be more effective. Effective communication in Krav Maga not only improves training and safety, but also carries over into everyday life. The ability to assertively communicate, use non-verbal cues effectively, and express oneself clearly and respectfully can greatly enhance personal and professional relationships.

Conclusion

Effective communication is an integral part of Krav Maga, enhancing training dynamics, conflict resolution, and interpersonal relationships. Through training, you learn how to express yourself assertively, read non-verbal cues, and improve your self-expression skills. These abilities extend beyond the training mat and positively impact personal and professional relationships. With enhanced communication skills, you have the power to navigate conflicts, set boundaries, and foster healthy connections in all areas of your life.

The communication skills developed through Krav Maga training allow individuals to confidently handle conflicts, express their needs, and collaborate with others in a respectful way. By practicing assertive communication, individuals build self-confidence and assert their rights and boundaries. This assertiveness extends beyond the training session, enabling individuals to advocate for themselves and make their voices heard in various situations. Whether it's asserting boundaries in personal relationships, expressing opinions at work, standing up against injustice, or achieving success in a sales role, the communication skills honed in Krav Maga empower individuals to assert themselves effectively.

CHAPTER 10

Relationships

"Relationships, much like Krav Maga, are built on trust. It's in the unspoken commitment to have each other's back, to defend, support, and uplift, that true bonds are forged."

Dr. GM Neil Farber

In Krav Maga, relationships matter just as much as the physical aspects of the training. Krav Maga emphasizes the value of working together and forming solid connections within the community. In this chapter, we will delve into how Krav Maga builds strong relationships through partner drills and training. We'll also discuss how it nurtures trust, teamwork, and cooperation, creating a healthy and supportive community..

Strengthening Bonds through Partner Drills

In Krav Maga, partner drills and training play a vital role. These exercises involve working closely with a training partner and simulating real-life self-defense situations. By practicing techniques together, you form strong relationships and build trust. This trust becomes the foundation for effective collaboration and cooperation. As you learn to rely on your training partners, a sense of camaraderie and shared goals develop. These shared experiences create a supportive community within the Krav Maga practice.

Partner drills foster a sense of accountability and responsibility towards one another. Each partner's safety and well-being become paramount, fostering an environment of care and mutual support. This mutual responsibility enhances your sense of trust and strengthens the relationships built through Krav Maga training.

"In Krav Maga partner drills, we find an eloquent dialogue of trust and resilience; teaching us that the strongest bonds are those tempered in the fires of shared challenge."

Fostering Trust, Teamwork, and Cooperation

Trust is crucial in any successful relationship, and Krav Maga training is the perfect way to build trust. Trust is built through repeated interactions, mutual support, and the understanding that both partners genuinely care about each other's well-being. As you train together, you gain confidence in your partner's abilities, which allows you to try new techniques and push yourselves further.

Teamwork and cooperation are vital in Krav Maga training. The effectiveness of techniques and self-defense strategies relies on partners working together seamlessly. By collaborating, you learn to communicate, move in sync, and anticipate each other's actions. This teamwork creates a sense of unity and reminds everyone of the importance of supporting and relying on one another.

> *"Krav Maga is a reminder that in the realm of relationships, it's not about overpowering or dominating, but about coexisting; balancing give and take, fostering trust and cooperation."*

Krav Maga promotes a non-competitive environment where people come together to learn and grow as a team. Instead of competing against each other, you cooperate and build a sense of community. By working together towards common goals and supporting each other's progress, you form strong relationships that go beyond training.

Nurturing Healthy Relationships within the Krav Maga Community

The Krav Maga community is a great place to flourish and develop. It's a special opportunity to connect with people who love self-defense and personal growth just like you. In this community, we build strong relationships through shared experiences, respect, and a dedication to each other's progress.

> *"Within the Krav Maga community, every punch, block, and grapple is more than just a technique; it's a handshake of trust, a nod of mutual respect, and a testament to the bonds we forge in shared dedication."*

Through such organizations like FIMA – The Federation of Israeli Martial Arts, the Krav Maga community serves as a network of support, encouragement, motivation, and education. Individuals uplift and inspire one another, celebrating successes and providing guidance during challenging times. The bonds formed within the Krav Maga community create a sense of belonging and foster a positive training environment.Members of the Krav Maga community come from various walks of life, united by their passion for self-defense and their commitment to personal growth. Within this diverse group, individuals find solace in the understanding that they are not alone in their journey. Whether a beginner seeking to build confidence or an experienced practitioner honing their skills, everyone is embraced with open arms and a shared purpose.

Through FIMA, the Krav Maga community extends its reach beyond national borders. FIMA brings together Krav Maga practitioners from around the world, creating a global network of like-minded individuals. Through regular seminars, workshops, and international events, they not only share their knowledge but also strengthen the bonds that tie them together. In these gatherings, seasoned instructors and practitioners share their experiences, techniques, and the latest developments in Krav Maga. The collective wisdom and camaraderie within the community generate an atmosphere of continuous learning and growth. No matter one's skill level, there is always something to be gained from the collective expertise of these passionate individuals.

What truly sets the FIMA Krav Maga family apart is its commitment to supporting one another outside of training sessions. When a member faces personal challenges or setbacks, the community stands ready to offer help and guidance. Whether it is offering a listening ear, practical advice, or moral support, everyone is invested in each other's well-being. While I am referring to FIMA here, realize that many other high quality organizations such as KMWW (Krav Maga Worldwide) with Darren Levine, IKMA (Israeli Krav Maga Association) with Haim Gidon, KMA (Krav Maga Alliance) with John Whitman, KMG (Krav Maga Global) with Eyal Yanilov, KMF-AC (Krav Maga Federation) with Alain Cohen, Dennis Hanover's Hisardut, Michael Ruppel's Street Defense, and many others, refer to and treat their students and members as part of their family. FIMA is the umbrella and larger home that brings all of these organizations and members into one bigger, extended family.

We also understand the importance of celebrating each other's successes. From the first time a beginner executes a technique flawlessly to the achievement of advanced ranks, each milestone is met with praise and admiration. Success is not seen as competition within the community but rather as something to be cherished and acknowledged collectively.

This spirit of support and celebration extends to the wider community as well. We often engage in charitable events, using our skills to raise funds and awareness for causes close to our hearts. For example, part of the proceeds to FIMA are donated to The Lone Soldier Program to support Israel. By coming together to contribute positively to society, we embody the principles of strength, compassion, and resilience that Krav Maga instills.

In this interconnected world, where isolation and divisiveness sometimes prevail, the FIMA Krav Maga family stands as a captivating example of unity and collaboration. Its members cherish the sense of belonging and genuine connections they have forged. Through their shared experiences, they reassure each other that no obstacle is insurmountable and that they are capable of overcoming anything through perseverance and mutual support.

As the FIMA Krav Maga family continues to grow and evolve, its influence extends beyond the realm of self-defense. It serves as a beacon of hope, reminding individuals of the incredible power found within human connection and shared passion. With each new practitioner welcomed into its folds, the community flourishes, leaving an indelible mark on the world as a testament to the strength of its bonds and the transformative power of unity.

Furthermore, the FIMA Krav Maga family offers opportunities for socialization and building friendships beyond the training sessions. Events, seminars, and gatherings provide platforms for you to connect on a personal level, sharing experiences and interests beyond self-defense. These social interactions deepen relationships and contribute to the overall well-being and enjoyment of being part of the Krav Maga community.

In Krav Maga, relationships are vital. They make training better, building trust, teamwork, and collaboration. They also create a strong community. By working with partners and doing drills, people form strong connections, which encourage trust and cooperation. Krav Maga emphasizes working together and supporting each other. This community fosters healthy relationships through shared experiences, respect, and a commitment to personal growth. Beyond training, these relationships provide a support system where partners offer guidance, encouragement, and motivation.

Having a strong support network is crucial during tough moments, and it positively impacts progress and well-being. Additionally, the FIMA Krav Maga family provides a place for socializing and making friends. Events and gatherings bring practitioners together, allowing personal connections to be formed. These interactions create opportunities to build lasting friendships, share experiences, and form relationships that go beyond training.

Within FIMA, like in many Krav Maga organizations, there is a shared understanding and respect for each other's journeys. The diversity of individuals, with different backgrounds, ages, and skill levels, contributes to a  rich and inclusive community. This inclusivity fosters an environment where everyone feels valued, accepted, and supported, regardless of their starting point or level of expertise..

Relationships outside of Krav Maga

The lessons learned in Krav Maga about relationships have a big impact outside of the training mat. Trust, an important part of successful relationships, is practiced and developed in Krav Maga through drills and teamwork. As you progress in your Krav Maga journey, you come to understand how important trust is in personal and professional relationships.

> *"Just as Krav Maga hones our instincts for defense, it nurtures our capacity for trust, respect, and compassion; foundations for healthy relationships in every arena of life."*

Many studies have shown that trust is crucial in relationships. Trust forms the basis for emotional closeness, creating feelings of safety, vulnerability, and respect. In personal relationships, whether with family, friends, or partners, trust is the foundation of a strong connection. You learn to rely on and trust your training partners, which also helps you build trust in your personal lives. This increased ability to trust can lead to more satisfying relationships, as you feel more comfortable sharing your emotions with your loved ones.

Trust is a crucial factor in professional relationships. When working together, colleagues must have faith in one another to accomplish shared objectives. The teamwork and cooperation fostered in Krav Maga training directly apply to effective communication and collaboration in the workplace. Krav Maga practitioners who have developed their trust-building skills are more likely to be given leadership positions and be recognized as dependable team members. This can open doors to better career prospects and greater professional achievements.

Krav Maga's impact on relationships is not solely based on trust. Krav Maga instills important values like respect, integrity, and empathy, which lead to healthier interactions with others. As you advance in your Krav Maga journey, you develop a stronger understanding of yourself, better control over your emotions, and greater empathy. These qualities improve your capacity to comprehend and connect with others, resulting in more fulfilling and positive relationships.

Developing and maintaining healthy relationships is essential for personal growth and happiness. When you surround yourself with supportive and empowering people, it has a positive impact on your self-esteem and overall well-being. Practicing Krav Maga can contribute to this by boosting your confidence and sense of empowerment, which can then have a positive effect on your relationships. It can help you feel more secure in expressing your needs and boundaries, communicating effectively, and finding fulfillment in your relationships.

Creating deep connections and building meaningful memories holds great importance in nurturing relationships. Within the Krav Maga community, you come together to train, expand your knowledge, and grow collectively. By facing challenges together, offering support and celebration during each other's progress, you cultivate a strong sense of camaraderie and empathy. This bond within the community strengthens connections and enhances overall personal happiness.

Krav Maga not only teaches self-defense, but it also helps us appreciate those who support us. Practicing gratitude is a powerful way to improve relationships, as it allows us to recognize the positive impact others have on our lives. In Krav Maga, we often thank our training partners, instructors, and fellow practitioners for their support and encouragement. This gratitude culture strengthens relationships and creates a positive training environment.

Apart from trust and gratitude, Krav Maga can also promote optimism in relationships. During training, you develop a growth mindset, seeing challenges as opportunities for growth. This mindset can extend to your relationships, helping you approach conflicts and obstacles with a more positive and problem-solving mindset.

The lessons learned in Krav Maga about relationships are invaluable. The emphasis on trust, teamwork, cooperation, and effective communication enhances personal and professional relationships, promoting understanding, trust, and mutual respect. You experience the benefits of healthy relationships through personal growth, sharing experiences, empowerment, gratitude, and optimism, creating a positive ripple effect in all aspects of your life.

Conclusion

Practicing partner drills and training together build trust, teamwork, and cooperation. These skills not only help us grow in Krav Maga but also in all areas of life. The Krav Maga community provides a supportive environment where we can develop healthy relationships, find inspiration, and make lasting friendships.

The relationships we build in Krav Maga contribute to personal growth and empowerment. Our training partners and fellow practitioners become a source of support, guidance, and feedback, pushing us to constantly improve. Seeing our own progress and the progress of others in the community inspires us to surpass our limits and strive for excellence.

Strong and trusting relationships outside of Krav Maga create a sense of safety and vulnerability, allowing for emotional intimacy and mutual respect. These bonds contribute to our overall well-being, providing a support system that encourages self-expression, personal growth, and the pursuit of fulfilling experiences.

In our personal relationships, trust and effective communication lead to deeper connections and healthier interactions. In the workplace, teamwork and cooperation strengthen professional relationships, leading to more collaborative and successful outcomes. Ultimately, building and nurturing strong relationships in all aspects of life have a positive impact on our mental health, promoting optimism, gratitude, and a sense of empowerment.

Krav Maga imparts valuable insights into the importance of relationships for personal growth and mental well-being. Trust and strong bonds formed within the Krav Maga community inspire individuals to strive for excellence in all their endeavors.

CHAPTER 11

Introspection

"Through Krav Maga, we find that the path to external strength is paved with introspection, for it's in truly knowing ourselves that we become undefeatable."

Dr. GM Neil Farber

Krav Maga offers a unique opportunity for introspection. In this chapter, we will dive into how Krav Maga serves as a powerful tool for self-reflection and self- discovery, we'll explore the significance of uncovering personal values, goals, and boundaries, and find out how the practice of Krav Maga enhances self-awareness and promotes personal growth.

Krav Maga as a Tool for Self-Reflection

Krav Maga training is a powerful and transformative experience. It pushes you to your limits, both physically and mentally. This intense practice challenges you to face your fears, overcome obstacles, and tap into your inner strength. Through this process, you are able to reflect on yourself and discover who you truly are.

During Krav Maga training, you are encouraged to delve deep into your motivations, fears, and strengths. You confront your limitations head-on and uncover your incredible resilience. By immersing yourself in the rigorous demands of Krav Maga, you gain valuable insights into your character, beliefs, and abilities.

> *"In the dance of Krav Maga, each movement isn't just an external expression; it's an invitation to delve deeper, to reflect upon our intentions, fears, and strengths."*

The intensity of Krav Maga creates the perfect environment for self-reflection. It allows you to observe how you react and respond under pressure. By carefully analyzing your emotions, thoughts, and behaviors in challenging situations, you can identify areas for personal growth. This self-reflection helps you develop effective strategies to overcome any obstacles you may encounter.

Krav Maga is a vehicle for personal growth and self-improvement. By pushing yourself outside of your comfort zone and facing your fears, you develop a greater understanding of yourself and those around you. This knowledge allows you to navigate life's challenges with confidence and resilience.

In addition, Krav Maga training builds mental fortitude and toughness. As you push through physically and mentally demanding exercises, you cultivate a sense of determination and perseverance that can be applied to any situation. This mental strength becomes a valuable asset in your everyday life, helping you overcome obstacles with ease.

Krav Maga also teaches you self-discipline and emotional control. In the midst of intense training scenarios, you must remain calm and composed. This practice translates into other areas of your life, enabling you to handle stressful situations more effectively.

Through the process of self-reflection and self-discovery, Krav Maga provides you with a deeper understanding of your own values and priorities. This self-awareness allows you to make more informed decisions that align with your personal goals.

Overall, Krav Maga offers a transformative journey of introspection, allowing you to develop a deeper understanding of yourself and become more equipped to face life's challenges with resilience and confidence. As you navigate through the chapters of this book, you may notice the repetition of important concepts. Rest assured, this is not an oversight. Rather, it is a deliberate inclusion, highlighting the interconnectedness of various facets of positive psychology within Krav Maga. Brace yourself, for as we progress further on this Krav Mind adventure, the interrelatedness will become even more apparent.

Exploring Personal Values, Goals, and Boundaries in Krav Maga

Krav Maga offers a unique opportunity for you to explore your own values, goals, and boundaries. By committing to the discipline and rigor of Krav Maga, you can align your actions with your values and gain a strong sense of purpose. The practice also helps you develop important qualities like perseverance, determination, and continuous improvement.

A crucial aspect of Krav Maga is understanding one's values. Through training, you are prompted to deeply reflect on what truly matters to you when it comes to self-protection and defending your loved ones. As you progress in your journey, you discover the core values that motivate you to pursue Krav Maga. By connecting your self-defense goals with these values, you can embark on a more meaningful and purposeful path. When personal values are at the forefront of self-defense goals, you become even more powerful and inspire people to surpass their limits, not just for themselves but for the safety of others.

> *"In the heat of Krav Maga training, the veneer of daily life melts away, revealing the core of our values, the authenticity of our aspirations, and the truth of our purpose."*

Goal setting in Krav Maga also highlights the importance of realistic and value-based objectives. As you progress in your training, you set challenging milestones that you can actually achieve in real-life self-defense situations. This approach ensures that self-defense goals are attainable, allowing you to make progress and feel accomplished. It also prevents frustration and helps maintain enthusiasm and dedication to the Krav Maga journey.

Additionally, viewing self-defense goals as necessities rather than mere desires helps strengthen commitment. When people see self-defense skills as essential for personal safety and that of others, they are more likely to invest time and effort into achieving them. Krav Maga training naturally promotes this mindset by instilling the belief that these skills are not just wanted, but necessary for self-defense and protection.

In Krav Maga, setting and respecting personal boundaries is just as important as achieving goals. By engaging in partner drills and simulations, you learn to understand and assert your limits for self-defense. This helps you become more aware of your boundaries and confidently communicate them during training and real-life situations, ensuring your safety. In Krav Maga, boundaries are crucial for effective and injury-free training. Clear communication of boundaries during partner drills allows both you to train safely and productively. Establishing and respecting physical and emotional boundaries with training partners promotes a culture of mutual respect and safety within the Krav Maga community.

The Introspection Advantage

Krav Maga helps you look within yourself, discover your values and goals, and become more self-aware. It helps you establish and communicate boundaries, leading to healthier relationships. By practicing Krav Maga, you gain insights into your motivations and strengths, and learn how to make conscious choices for personal growth.

> *"Beyond defense, Krav Maga is a dialogue with the self, a profound exploration of our limits, our aspirations, and the uncharted terrains of our inner landscapes."*

Krav Maga is a path towards personal growth and self-improvement. By adopting a growth mindset, you see mistakes and setbacks as opportunities to learn and get better. This mindset makes you resilient, adaptable, and ready to face new challenges.

In Krav Maga, there is a continuous progression that pushes you to push your limits and strive for improvement. By constantly challenging yourself, you become more self-aware and gain a deeper understanding of who you are and how you function. You become aware of your strengths, weaknesses, triggers, and patterns of behavior in all areas of your life.

Engaging in Krav Maga training helps you become more aware of your body. You learn to recognize and use your physical abilities, becoming more in tune with your body and its potential. This improved body awareness benefits your overall physical health. One example of this is proprioception, which is knowing where your body is in space and how it moves. During training, you practice specific movements that require precision and coordination. By repeatedly performing these movements, you become more attuned to your body's position and motion. This heightened body awareness not only improves your performance in Krav Maga but also benefits other activities like sports, dance, or simply moving confidently in crowded spaces.

In Krav Maga, body awareness goes beyond just physical skills. It also involves being able to recognize how your body reacts to stress. During intense training, you become more aware of things like your increased heart rate, shallow breathing, and muscle tension. By understanding these signs, you can learn to manage stress better and stay calm in high-pressure situations outside of Krav Maga, like public speaking or job interviews.

Krav Maga also helps you become more self-aware, both emotionally and physically. This deeper understanding of yourself can lead to overall wellbeing and personal growth. It gives you a sense of empowerment and control over your life, making it easier to handle challenges, make decisions, and pursue your goals with confidence and resilience.

Krav Maga helps build mental and emotional strength by facing and overcoming challenges. It teaches you how to manage stress, control your emotions, and stay focused even in difficult situations. These skills are not only useful in self-defense situations but also in everyday life.

Moreover, Krav Maga encourages personal growth. As you train, you set new goals, push yourself, and work towards self-improvement. Learning and perfecting techniques helps develop a growth mindset, where you see mistakes as chances to learn and grow.

Conclusion

When you engage in Krav Maga, you embark on a journey of self-reflection, self-awareness, and self-discovery. By consistently practicing Krav Maga and overcoming its challenges, you gain valuable insights into your motivations, fears, strengths, and limitations. This introspection allows you to deepen your understanding of yourself, mentally and physically. It encourages you to develop a growth mindset and resilience.

The benefits of this enhanced self-awareness positively impacts various aspects of your life, including your overall well-being, relationships, and pursuit of personal goals. By embracing introspection as an integral part of your Krav Maga journey, you can continually evolve, adapt, and thrive in both self-defense situations and everyday life challenges.

Krav Maga offers a transformative experience. It helps you tap into your inner strength, gain clarity about your values and goals, and cultivate a strong sense of self-awareness. With Krav Maga as your guide, you become empowered to face any obstacle with confidence and resilience.

CHAPTER 12

Mind-Body Connection

"Krav Maga teaches us that the ultimate defense is a mind and body in perfect harmony, attuned to each other, moving as one in the face of any challenge."

Dr. GM Neil Farber

In Krav Maga, the Mind-Body Connection is a key factor that highlights how our physical and mental health are closely intertwined. This chapter investigates the significant influence of this connection and emphasizes the need for a harmonious mind-body relationship to fully reap the mental rewards of practicing Krav Maga.

What is a Mind – Body Connection?

The mind-body connection refers to the interrelation and interaction between your mental and emotional state (mind) and your physical well-being and bodily functions (body). This is one of the most important connections that we have in our lives. Many skeptics might hear "mind-body connection" and think we're discussing "new age guru" stuff. This isn't the case. The mind-body connection is something that we each experience every single day. Here are several examples that you may recognize:

- Goosebumps forming when you experience strong emotions.
- Feeling a rush of adrenaline when a car is coming toward you.
- Wretch violently at the sign of maggots in the trash.
- Salivating at the sight of a lemon.
- Feeling your heart rate increase when you're excited or anxious.
- Blushing when you're embarrassed or shy.
- Feeling your stomach churn when you're nervous or anxious.
- Sweating when you're nervous or stressed.
- Developing a tension headache when under stress.
- Feeling your muscles tense up when faced with a threat or danger.
- Feeling your breath quicken during intense fear.
- Feeling weak or shaky when you're extremely hungry or fatigued.
- Developing a racing mind or insomnia due to stress or anxiety.
- Developing digestive discomfort during stressful times.
- Feeling euphoria or runner's high after intense physical exercise.
- Experiencing a sense of calm and relaxation during deep breathing.

We know that mental and psychological stress can damage the body. It's healing the body and optimizing function and performance that we want to focus on. There is an abundance of scientific research that shows the mind has incredible powers over the body. Nine specific examples of this are:

1. Placebo effect - when believing that a treatment will work actually makes you feel better, even if the treatment itself doesn't have any real medical effect. For example, patients having fake back surgery for back pain, had dramatic improvements.
2. Nocebo effect - opposite of placebo effect. Negative beliefs bring about negative outcomes when there's no physical reason for them to happen.
3. Mindful meditation reduces the perception of pain and improves pain-related outcomes.
4. Managing stress through techniques like relaxation and meditation improve heart health and reduce risk of heart disease.
5. Cognitive-behavioral interventions are effective in reducing chronic pain and improving quality of life.
6. Athletes using mental imagery and visualization techniques experience enhanced performance and improved recovery from injuries.
7. Meditation protects against depression and exercise is a great treatment for depression.
8. Beliefs and thoughts ease pain, more quickly heal wounds, improve your immune system and even slow the progression of some cancers.
9. Social connections and an optimistic outlook are associated with longer life expectancy.

Don't be a skeptic. We know that a strong mind-body connection exists. What we want to understand is how Krav Maga fosters this connection and how can we maintain better control of this powerful association.

Physical and Mental Well-Being in Krav Maga

Krav Maga emphasizes the connection between our physical actions and mental state. Numerous experts, including Darren Levine, Itay Gil, David Kahn, Eyal Yanilov, John Whitman, Moti Horenstein, Tommi Nystrom, Alain Cohen, and others have discussed how intensive physical training not only strengthens your body but also profoundly affects your mind. By pushing your limits, you develop mental strength and resilience beyond the training session.

Finding a balance between your mind and body is essential for optimal performance and overall well-being. A clear and focused mind improves the effectiveness of your physical techniques, while a healthy body supports mental clarity and emotional stability. By embracing the link between your mind and body, you unlock hidden potential and take your Krav Maga skills to new levels.

> *"Krav Maga is the harmonious union of mind and body, where every movement becomes a meditation, every defense a deepened understanding."*

Breath and Movement Synchronization is a powerful technique that has a great impact on both performance and mental well-being. When we align our breath with physical actions like striking, blocking, kicking, and evading, we create a smooth and balanced rhythm. This not only benefits your physical strength and agility, but also has a profound effect on your mind. By focusing on your breath and movements, you sharpen your concentration and become more mindful of the present moment. This helps you let go of past failures and future uncertainties, enabling you to fully concentrate on what you're doing right now. Moreover, when faced with challenges, being able to control your breath strengthens your mental resilience.

Mindful training: By staying present, you enhance your understanding of what you can do and become better at controlling yourself and managing your emotions. Instead of letting stress dictate your actions, you learn to respond with careful consideration and composure. This ability to stay in control 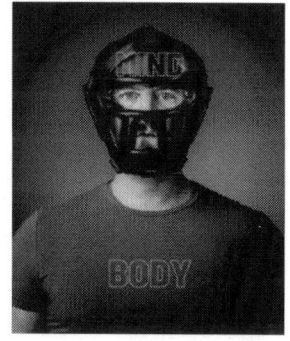 is priceless, as it allows you to think logically and make quick decisions when faced with intense situations in any area of your life.

Visualization: When you mentally practice something, it actually helps your body remember how to do it, activates the same neural pathways as physical practice, and makes you feel more confident. Visualizing yourself doing things well helps strengthen the connection between your mind and body. It also helps you believe in yourself and approach any kind of training or real-life situation with a positive attitude. By mentally overcoming challenges, you become mentally strong and ready to face difficult times with bravery and determination.

Rest and Recovery: Rest isn't just about physical recovery; it also allows the mind to process and integrate the experiences from training sessions. Reflecting on successes and challenges during rest periods helps you learn and grow, refining techniques and strategies. Moreover, rest and recovery are essential for maintaining the mind-body balance. By prioritizing rest, you ensure that you're mentally and physically prepared to engage fully in your Krav Maga practice, unlocking your true potential.

Forging a Strong Mind-Body Connection

To forge a strong mind-body connection, dedicate time during each training session to focus on your breath, ensuring it remains steady and controlled throughout various drills and techniques.

Mindful breathing: Incorporating deep, diaphragmatic breathing into your daily routine goes beyond just training sessions. Whenever you feel stressed or tense, practicing this technique can help you feel more composed, calm, and mentally well.

Meditation and Visualization: Meditation is an invaluable tool for fostering mental focus and cultivating mindfulness. Regular meditation practice helps you develop a heightened awareness of your thoughts and emotions, facilitating better self-control and decision-making both in training and real-life situations.

Darren Levine was one of the first Krav Maga instructors to write about incorporating a brief meditation practice before, during, and after your Krav Maga training sessions. As Darren has described this, each meditation session encompasses a very different aspect of awareness and insight. Before the training, your meditation (1-10 minutes) is thought provoking and readying your mind and body for the workout. It may be guided (and I would add visualize some of the scenarios, if known, which you will practice in class). During the class, mindfulness meditation during practice (and I would add, additional visualization of scenarios you are working on) will help calm, center your focus and bring awareness to the forefront of everything you do. After class, is the time for calming the mind, gratitude, contemplative and insight meditation as a thoughtful review of your experiences.

> *"In the pulse of Krav Maga, the mind doesn't just direct the body; they dance together, forging a connection that transcends technique, illuminating the power of unified intent."*

Just as traditional meditation ands mindfulness meditation are important for building the mind-body connection, visualization is also essential. By dedicating time to mentally rehearsing different scenarios and picturing ourselves executing techniques flawlessly, handling challenges, and effectively overcoming opponents, we strengthen our muscle memory and boost our confidence. This reinforces the connection between our mind and body. Eyal Yanilov emphasizes the use of this technique in training his students to develop a "Combat mindset".

Mindful Training Partnerships: In training sessions, remember to do more than just perform techniques. Take the time to closely observe your training partners and how they move and react. By being fully present and paying attention to their actions, you can improve your own skills and adjust to various situations as they unfold. This shared focus encourages effective communication and helps you develop a greater understanding of the mind-body connection, both within yourself and in others.

Incorporating Mental Exercises into Krav Maga training strengthens the mind-body connection. For example, you can engage in concentration drills where you maintain unwavering focus on specific targets or engage in mental stimulations of various self-defense scenarios. In order to excel in Krav Maga and other aspects of life, it is important to have a focused and determined mindset. This can be achieved through mental exercises and visualizing the successful achievement of personal goals. By incorporating mindful breathing, meditation, visualization, and mental exercises into training and everyday life, you can develop a strong connection between your mind and body. This journey not only enhances performance in Krav Maga, but also promotes mental well-being and personal growth. These strategies allow you to approach challenges with calmness and make informed decisions under pressure. Ultimately, striving for a strong mind-body connection is a means to becoming a master of Krav Maga and discovering inner strength.

The Wonders of Mental and Physical Balance

The mind-body connection developed through Krav Maga training offers remarkable benefits that extend beyond the training mat, positively impacting various aspects of your life outside of the gym.

> *"In the equilibrium of mental and physical balance, we discover the profound magic of wholeness; where every thought finds its movement, and every step is infused with intent."*

Let's explore some examples of how to apply these categories to daily personal life, professional life, interactions, relationships, and more:

Emotional Resilience and Stress Management: Achieving emotional resilience and effectively handling stress requires a delicate equilibrium between mental and physical well-being. By honing mindful training and breath control techniques, you gain the ability to navigate feelings of fear, anxiety, and other intense emotions that often arise during high-stress circumstances. By acknowledging and understanding your emotional responses, you develop the skill of maintaining composure and making logical decisions when the pressure is on. This invaluable emotional resilience can prove crucial in real-life situations, whether it's ensuring your survival or coping with work challenges and managing intricate relationships.

Personal Life: When dealing with a tough personal situation, such as a difficult conversation with someone you care about, you can apply mindful breathing techniques to stay calm and emotionally balanced. By staying in the moment and controlling your feelings, you can approach the conversation with thoughtfulness and handle any conflicts in a positive way.

Professional Life: In a demanding work setting, practicing mindfulness can help you concentrate on your work and make better choices. By using controlled breathing techniques, you can effectively manage stress while giving a presentation or attending a meeting, ensuring that you think clearly and communicate successfully.

Relationships: In a fiery dispute with a loved one, you can tap into the emotional strength gained from practicing Krav Maga to avoid rash responses. By recognizing and dealing with your feelings, you can react with compassion and comprehension, which promotes better communication and stronger bonds.

Mental Wellness and Personal Growth: Achieving mental balance through mindful training and visualization allows you to confront fears, overcome self-doubt, and foster self-belief. This newfound mental strength positively impacts many areas of your life. Through the challenges of Krav Maga, you'll build resilience, discipline, and determination, which will boost your self-confidence and give you the mindset of a warrior. As you achieve mastery and advance in skill levels, you will experience a sense of accomplishment that will nurture a positive and empowered attitude in all aspects of your life. This newfound mental wellness will help you grow personally and face challenges with determination and optimism..

- **Personal Life**: Visualization is a powerful tool that can help you achieve your goals and create success. By imagining yourself reaching your desired outcomes and preparing for important events, you can increase your self-confidence and drive. This mental practice will enable you to overcome challenges and accomplish your goals.

- **Professional Life**: Applying mental imagery during career advancement can enhance your confidence in interviews or important meetings. By visualizing yourself excelling in various scenarios, you build self-assurance and a positive attitude that sets the stage for success.
- **Relationships**: Building mental strength through Krav Maga helps you tackle insecurities and fears that may hold you back from personal growth. Embracing self-confidence enables you to be more open to self-improvement and forge stronger bonds with others.

Enhanced Focus and Concentration: Incorporating mindfulness training and breath control into your life can greatly improve your ability to stay present and focused. By practicing mindful breathing during stressful moments, you can regain a sense of calm and composure. This in turn allows you to think clearly and make informed decisions, even in high-pressure situations. With heightened focus and concentration, you can excel in your work, maintain fulfilling relationships, and approach tasks more efficiently and effectively.

- **Personal Life**: Mindful training translates to better focus on hobbies or personal projects. By immersing yourself fully in activities, you'll experience greater enjoyment and satisfaction, leading to a sense of accomplishment in various pursuits.
- **Professional Life**: Maintaining focus and concentration at work helps you complete tasks efficiently and improve productivity. By minimizing distractions and staying present in your work responsibilities, you'll

achieve better results and feel more fulfilled in your career.
- **Interactions**: During conversations with others, applying attentive listening fosters a deeper understanding of their perspectives and feelings. By fully engaging in all your interactions, you can build trust and strengthen connections in both personal and professional relationships.

Improved Communication and Relationships: The mind-body connection in Krav Maga training affects all relationships. When you're fully present and focused during training, carefully observing your partners' actions and reactions, you develop excellent communication skills and gain a better understanding of others. This attentive mindset helps you cultivate empathy, actively listen, and treat others with respect in all areas of your life. By maintaining a balanced mind-body connection, you enhance your ability to communicate effectively, handle conflicts in a positive way, and build more meaningful and fulfilling relationships.

- **Personal Life**: Applying the communication skills developed in Krav Maga, such as assertiveness and active listening, can improve relationships with family members and friends. By expressing your needs and boundaries clearly, you establish healthier dynamics and more meaningful connections.
- **Professional Life**: In the workplace, effective communication with colleagues and superiors helps build a positive work environment. By actively listening to others' ideas and concerns, you can foster a collaborative atmosphere that benefits team projects and overall productivity.

- **Interactions**: The mind-body connection enables you to read and respond to non-verbal cues, improving your ability to empathize with others' emotions and perspectives. This heightened emotional intelligence facilitates more authentic and empathetic interactions.

Resilience in the Face of Challenges: Krav Maga's emphasis on mental and physical resilience empowers you to face life's challenges with courage and determination. The mindset of confronting and overcoming challenges that you develop in training extends to all areas of your life. You'll be more adaptable, learning to embrace change and adversity with confidence. The mental strength cultivated in Krav Maga enables you to bounce back from setbacks, learn from failures, and persist in pursuing your goals.

- **Personal Life**: Facing personal setbacks or obstacles, such as health issues or financial difficulties, you can draw upon the resilience developed in Krav Maga to adapt and persevere. The ability to confront challenges with determination and a growth mindset helps you navigate life's uncertainties with greater confidence.
- **Professional Life**: Confronting work-related challenges, such as tight deadlines or unexpected setbacks, you can employ problem-solving skills developed through Krav Maga. By seeing challenges as opportunities for learning and growth, you can approach them with a solutions-oriented mindset.
- **Relationships**: Applying resilience in relationships involves embracing conflicts as opportunities for growth and understanding. By viewing disagreements

as a chance to improve communication and deepen connections, you can navigate relationship challenges with a positive and constructive outlook.

The mind and body are deeply connected, and understanding this connection is crucial to unlocking the full potential of Krav Maga for self-defense and mental wellbeing. By recognizing the significance of mental focus, emotional strength, and physical abilities, you can achieve a harmonious balance that empowers you to face challenges with certainty, confront fears with bravery, and embrace personal growth with determination. Krav Maga has a profound impact on the mind-body connection, making it a comprehensive system for self-improvement and mental resilience, both in the gym and in all areas of your life.

Conclusion

In this chapter, we explore the powerful connection between the mind and body in Krav Maga. It goes far beyond simply physical training, as we discover the amazing ways in which our thoughts and movements work together. Throughout these pages, we learn about the importance of breathing in sync with our actions, practicing mindfulness, using visualization, and taking time to rest and recover.

This mind-body connection in Krav Maga goes beyond just learning techniques. It has the power to transform us completely, both mentally and physically. As we dive deeper into this connection, we develop emotional resilience, sharpen our focus, and become more self-aware. We begin to unlock the true potential of Krav Maga's mental benefits.

But the impact of this connection doesn't stop on the training mat. The lessons we learn here carry over into our everyday lives, giving us the confidence and strength to tackle challenges head-on. By facing our fears, overcoming adversity, and managing stress, we gain an incredible sense of self-assurance. With these tools, we can navigate the complexities of life with greater ease and grace.

Krav Maga helps you connect your mind and body, making you more self-aware and emotionally intelligent. This connection allows you to become a warrior in Krav Maga and in your personal growth and mental well-being. By embarking on this transformative journey, you unlock the true potential of your inner warrior and forge a powerful bond between your mind and body. This enriches your life in immeasurable ways.

CHAPTER 13

Embracing Fear

"Fear is the path to the dark side. Fear leads to anger, anger leads to hate, hate leads to suffering."

Yoda (Star Wars)

Fear is a natural and instinctive feeling that helps us stay safe by warning us about possible dangers. In this chapter we explore how Krav Maga offers a special opportunity to face and conquer our fears. and overcome your fears. By doing so, it allows us to turn fear into a powerful source of inner strength and the ability to bounce back.

Confronting and Overcoming Fears

In Krav Maga, fear is not brushed aside or ignored, but rather embraced as a chance to develop and uncover one's true potential. The training setting replicates actual-life circumstances, frequently incorporating confrontations and potentially risky situations. When you confront these challenges head-on, it's normal for fear to emerge.

"Every fear confronted is a mountain scaled, a lesson learned, and a testament to the indomitable spirit that resides within us all."

Rather than letting fear paralyze you, acknowledge its presence and explore its roots. By understanding why you are afraid, you can gain insights into your thought patterns, past experiences, and limiting beliefs. This self-reflection is the foundation for using fear as a catalyst for personal development. Krav Maga training takes a systematic approach to confronting fear. Techniques and scenarios are introduced in a controlled environment, giving you the opportunity to gradually build competence and confidence. With repeated practice, you will become more familiar with the situations that trigger fear, thereby reducing its intensity over time.

In the world of Krav Maga, fear is seen as a powerful ally. Instead of being overwhelmed by it, practitioners are taught to use fear to their advantage. By harnessing fear, one can become more aware of their surroundings and better able to make decisions in tricky situations. Facing fear head-on allows individuals to break down personal barriers and grow in confidence. This shift in mindset transforms fear from a weakness to a strength, enabling individuals to face challenges with courage and strategic thinking.

Managing Anxiety during High-Stress Situations

One of the key tools in managing fear and anxiety during high-stress situations is breath control. Deep and controlled breathing helps calm the nervous system, reducing the body's stress response and promoting emotional regulation.

> *"In the face of fear, we don't merely discover who we are; we shape who we become—braving the shadows to emerge brighter, bolder, and unbroken."*

By focusing on your breath in moments of high intensity, you can ground yourself in the present and prevent your mind from going into a spiral of panic or self-doubt. This sense of centeredness allows you to think more clearly, accurately assess threats, and respond strategically.

In the practice of Krav Maga, there is a strong emphasis on cultivating positive self-talk and affirmations as a means to overcome self-doubt and negative thought patterns. Throughout training, instructors encourage students to replace fear-based thoughts with empowering statements. For instance, instead of saying "I can't do this," they encourage saying "I am capable and strong." Similarly, asking the question "How will I do this?" opens up the possibility for exploring new ways of approaching challenges.

Krav Maga visualization techniques are essential for conquering fear and anxiety. Through mental rehearsal, you imagine yourself confidently tackling challenging situations and executing techniques flawlessly. This practice helps build confidence and prepares your mind for action. By mentally navigating potential obstacles beforehand, you approach high-stress scenarios with a sense of readiness. This preparation allows you to respond effectively and maintain composure.

Krav Maga's emphasis on realistic scenario training prepares you for real-life encounters. By simulating threatening situations during training, practitioners become acclimated to the rush of adrenaline and fear that may arise in actual self-defense scenarios. Realistic scenario training allows you to confront and overcome your fears in a controlled and supportive environment. With each successful execution of techniques in training, you build a reservoir of positive experiences that bolster your confidence and readiness for real-life situations.

Managing fear and anxiety during stressful situations is a crucial skill you can learn through Krav Maga training. By using techniques like controlling your breath, having positive thoughts, visualizing success, and practicing realistic scenarios, you can strengthen your mental resilience. This will help you face fear directly and stay calm in difficult circumstances.

Facing fears in daily life

In the world of Krav Maga, overcoming fears is a powerful way to push yourself beyond your limits. By facing physical and psychological challenges, you build resilience that can be applied to all areas of your life. This newfound strength allows you to tackle obstacles and pursue your goals with unwavering determination.

> *"Fears are life's invitations—to grow, to evolve, to stand tall. In overcoming them, we don't just survive; we thrive, becoming beacons of hope and pillars of inspiration."*

Krav Maga serves as a transformative path for embracing fear and transforming it into a source of empowerment. By acknowledging your fears, gradually exposing yourself to challenges, and using fear as a tool for growth, you cultivate mental resilience and enhance your self-confidence. Confronting and conquering fears within the controlled environment of Krav Maga sets the stage for personal development and equips you with the courage and adaptability needed to face the uncertainties of life. Ultimately, embracing fear becomes a defining aspect of your Krav Maga journey, unveiling the inner strength necessary to overcome both physical and mental barriers..

In Krav Maga training, facing your fears can have a profound impact on your daily life. As you conquer your fears again and again, your self-confidence soars. This newfound confidence spills over into all areas of your life. By proving to yourself that you can handle high-pressure situations and step outside your comfort zone, you start to believe in your ability to tackle challenges in everyday life.

Krav Maga provides a safe space for you to confront adversity and push through discomfort. The resilience you develop in training becomes a valuable tool when facing challenges outside the gym. The mental strength you gain from dealing with simulated threats and stressful scenarios prepares you to handle real-life obstacles with calmness and determination. Instead of seeing fear as an impossible barrier, you embrace it as a chance to grow and take action. This shift in perspective allows you to face fear with bravery and curiosity, recognizing it as a natural part of life's journey.

The problem-solving skills you learn in Krav Maga can be applied to everyday life. By thinking critically and making quick decisions under pressure, you'll be better prepared to handle unexpected challenges at work, in relationships, and in various other situations. Krav Maga also teaches adaptability, so you can confidently face uncertainties with creativity.

Facing fear in Krav Maga helps you regulate your emotions and manage stress. By learning to control fear during training, you'll develop emotional resilience that carries over into your daily life. When you encounter stress or conflicts outside of the gym, you'll be able to respond calmly and thoughtfully instead of reacting impulsively.

Embracing fear in personal life situations means taking charge of your life and making decisions that align with your values and aspirations. For instance, someone who has conquered their fear of public speaking through the mental training techniques of Krav Maga might now feel more confident speaking up in a work meeting or delivering a presentation to a large group. Embracing the fear of vulnerability can also lead to honest conversations in personal relationships, fostering deeper connections. It can also help in facing other fears, like skydiving or encountering snakes, as once you know how to conquer one fear, you can conquer others easily.

Practicing positive self-talk is important in high-stress situations outside of training. By affirming your own beliefs and building confidence, you can counteract the doubts that fear brings and maintain self-assurance.

Confronting fears and overcoming challenges in Krav Maga empowers you to take control of your life. When you realize that you have the strength to face and conquer your fears, this empowerment translates to all areas of your life. It fuels a proactive approach to obstacles and encourages personal growth and self-improvement.

In the professional world, the ability to make quick decisions, honed through Krav Maga training, can be applied to succeed in negotiations, crisis management, and problem-solving. For instance, a business executive who has developed quick decision-making skills in simulated self-defense scenarios can use that mental agility to make swift and well-thought-out choices in high-pressure business situations.

By facing fear in a controlled and supportive environment like Krav Maga, you can enhance your overall well-being, leading to personal growth and a strong belief in your ability to thrive in challenging situations. This transformation goes beyond the training mat, giving you the confidence and determination needed to conquer both internal and external obstacles.

The courage, self-assurance, resilience, and problem-solving skills gained from Krav Maga become guiding forces as you navigate through life. By embracing fear in this environment, you can improve your well-being, grow personally, and develop an unwavering belief in your ability to overcome adversity. This transformative impact extends beyond training, enabling you to tackle both internal and external challenges with courage and determination.

The tools learned in Krav Maga not only enhance self-defense capabilities but also improves your emotional well-being and personal growth. These techniques can be applied to everyday life, allowing you to handle stressful situations, make good decisions under pressure, and approach challenges with confidence. By embracing fear through Krav Maga, you will gain valuable life skills that empower you to overcome obstacles and live a fulfilling and resilient life.

Conclusion

In this chapter, we delve into the importance of fear in Krav Maga and how it can impact all areas of life. By facing fears and challenges in a controlled environment, Krav Maga practitioners develop mental resilience, self-confidence, and adaptability. These skills empower them to confront the uncertainties of life with bravery, turning fear into a source of strength.

The ability to embrace fear has a wide range of benefits, from making quick decisions under pressure in professional settings to fostering positive self-talk and vulnerability in personal relationships. Embracing fear becomes a guiding force for personal growth and success. It's not just about self-defense; it's about tapping into inner strength and tackling life's challenges with determination and unwavering belief. Krav Maga serves as a platform to discover the Warrior Within, leading to a fulfilling and empowered life beyond the training mat.

CHAPTER 14

Visualization

"Before the strike, before the defense, there's the vision. In Krav Maga, the art of visualization transforms imagination into instinct, and possibilities into powerful, precise action."

Dr. GM Neil Farber

In this chapter, we delve into the incredible ability of mental imagery to boost your confidence and belief in yourself. Through visualization, a technique widely used in Krav Maga, you can greatly improve your performance and mental resilience. By harnessing the power of visualization, you can conquer self-doubt and unlock your true potential.

Increased Confidence and Self-Efficacy

Visualization is all about creating strong mental images of yourself doing things well, dealing with opponents, and overcoming difficulties. When you visualize, your brain reacts in the same way as if you were physically doing those things, which helps to strengthen your muscle memory and boost your confidence.

> *"In Krav Maga, to visualize is to empower—to see beyond the present, to anticipate the next move, and to navigate the fluid dynamics of self-defense with clarity and confidence."*

With visualization, you can fully involve yourself in your training and self-defense situations without having to physically go through them. This type of mental practice allows you to repeat things over and over again, allowing you to improve your techniques and become really familiar with different situations.

Renowned Krav Maga master instructors such as Darren Levine, John Whitman, Itay Gil, David Kahn, Eyal Yanilov, Haim Gidon, Moti Horenstein, Alain Cohen, Ron Rotem, Guy Rafaeli, Nir Maman, Raphy Elgrissi, and Dennis Hanover, among others, firmly believe that incorporating visualization into training is crucial for enhancing combat readiness. Eyal Yanilov and Krav Maga Global specifically consider visualization as an essential and regular part of their training process to complement physical techniques.

Eyal Yanilov encourages his students to visualize a violent attack, initially imagining themselves losing. With each repetition, they visualize the attack again and refine their posture, strategies, techniques, and ultimate outcome until they emerge as the victors. Through visualizing successful execution of techniques and handling threatening situations, practitioners develop a stronger sense of self-confidence. Experiencing the initial loss mentally reduces the fear of injury and enhances their ability to perform under pressure. By mentally experiencing success, individuals can overcome self-doubt and believe in their own capabilities. This newfound confidence extends beyond the training environment and positively influences their approach to real-life challenges.

Visualization helps to build a positive self-image, where you see yourself as strong and capable of facing challenges with confidence. This self-belief makes you less affected by doubts or criticism from others.

Self-efficacy is the belief in your ability to achieve goals and overcome obstacles. In Krav Maga, visualization is important for increasing self-efficacy. When you imagine yourself successfully mastering techniques and dealing with threats, your belief in your skills and effectiveness improves.

With higher self-efficacy, you approach training and real-life situations with a positive attitude and the belief that you can succeed. You are more willing to push your limits, take on challenges, and make calculated risks. This mindset helps you learn and perform better because you view obstacles as opportunities for growth rather than impossible barriers.

Visualization is a powerful tool that can help you cope with performance anxiety in high-pressure situations. By mentally practicing techniques and imagining different scenarios, you become more familiar with the feelings and emotions you might experience. This familiarity reduces the element of surprise and fear of the unknown, helping you stay emotionally stable and composed in real-life situations. When I mention performance anxiety, I mean any situation where you are under pressure, such as asking someone on a date, performing on stage, demonstrating a technique in front of a class, or giving a business presentation. Visualization helps you mentally prepare for these challenging situations, giving you a sense of readiness and confidence. This mental preparation reduces the impact of performance anxiety, allowing you to perform at your best even when the stakes are high.

By using visualization and mental rehearsal, you can develop a strong sense of confidence and approach challenges with determination and resilience. This positive self-image then carries over to all areas of your life. When incorporating visualization into your Krav Maga practice, you tap into your untapped potential and embrace your inner warrior, ready to face any obstacles with unwavering assurance and self-belief.

Stress Reduction and Emotional Resilience

Visualization is a powerful tool for managing stress and building inner strength. It helps you stay calm and stable in the face of adversity. When life gets overwhelming, you can close your eyes and imagine yourself in a peaceful and empowering place. This mental escape helps you relax and recharge.

> *"In the midst of life's tumult, Krav Maga's practice of visualization offers a serene reprieve; where stress is transformed into strength, and worries yield to warrior-like clarity."*

Visualizing can also help you maintain a level-headed approach to difficult situations. By mentally stepping back and observing yourself in various scenarios, you gain a more objective perspective. This allows you to analyze problems more rationally and make logical decisions, rather than letting your emotions take over.

Visualizing yourself remaining composed, confident, and in control during high-pressure situations can also reinforce these positive responses in your subconscious mind. This fosters emotional resilience and helps you approach challenges with confidence, even when there is uncertainty or danger.

Visualization can help you manage your emotions in both training and real-life situations. By picturing yourself handling emotions effectively during practice, you can stay focused and calm even when faced with aggression or fear. This control over your feelings builds emotional resilience and enables you to respond well in difficult circumstances.

In Krav Maga, visualization is especially beneficial for reducing stress and boosting emotional strength. By creating a mental safe space, detaching yourself emotionally, reinforcing coping mechanisms, and improving emotional control, visualization equips you to handle life's challenges with composure and flexibility. It goes beyond physical techniques, transforming the way your mind and body work together and empowering you to approach problems with a balanced and centered mindset. Through this transformative mental practice, you can tap into your inner warrior, capable of facing fear, managing stress, and confronting obstacles with unwavering emotional stability.

In both your personal and professional life, you can use this relaxation technique to find a momentary break from the stress of your job, your family, or significant other. Instead of letting your emotions take over, you can mentally transport yourself to a peaceful beach or any calming place you enjoy.

This will have a positive effect on your heart rate, breathing, and even blood pressure. Take this chance to gradually return to reality and approach the situation with a fresh and emotionally strong perspective.

Enhanced Focus and Concentration

Visualization is a powerful tool that can sharpen your mind and help you stay focused during intense training sessions, real-life self-defense situations, and high-stress moments. It involves actively picturing yourself performing techniques and overcoming challenges in great detail. Regularly practicing visualization conditions your mind to be fully present and attentive to the task at hand.

> *"In the mindful practice of Krav Maga, visualization becomes our sanctuary; a haven where stress dissolves, replaced by the serene dance of foresight and focus."*

In the fast-paced world of Krav Maga training, it's easy to get sidetracked by distractions. Visualization helps you train your mind to block out external disturbances and maintain concentration on your objectives. By mentally rehearsing techniques and self-defense scenarios, you create a mental shield against distractions, allowing you to stay centered and undeterred by your surroundings. This heightened focus not only improves your learning efficiency but also gives you a greater sense of control in high-pressure situations, whether or not they involve self-defense.

In many professions, such as working on assembly lines, in nuclear power stations, or in counter-terror training, it is crucial to be fully present and focused. Visualization techniques, inspired by Krav Maga, can help us achieve this state of enhanced focus and productivity.

Visualization is key to achieving a state of "flow," where we are fully engaged in our actions, with heightened awareness and a sense of being in the zone. In this state, time seems to fly by and everything falls into place because we have the necessary skills to accomplish our tasks. However, it is important to strike a balance - if the tasks are too difficult, they can cause stress and fatigue, while tasks that are too easy can lead to boredom.

By practicing visualization, we can intentionally trigger this state of flow. By envisioning ourselves executing techniques flawlessly and handling complex situations with ease, we can better prepare ourselves to enter this heightened state of focus and performance in real-life scenarios.

Visualization helps you improve your decision-making abilities under pressure. By repeatedly simulating scenarios and mentally exploring different responses, you develop a repertoire of effective reactions to various threats, be they self-defense related or mental/emotional threats unrelated to Krav Maga. Here are some examples:

In Krav Maga:

Self-Defense Scenarios: At Krav Maga training, you imagine different self-defense situations, like someone sneaking up on you or trying to grab a weapon. By mentally practicing how to respond and picturing yourself successfully defending against the threat, you build up a collection of reliable reactions. When confronted with a real-life self-defense scenario, this mental preparation helps you react without thinking and make fast, smart choices.

Multiple Attackers: In Krav Maga, we often imagine scenarios where we are faced with multiple attackers. By mentally rehearsing these situations, we train ourselves to be aware of our surroundings, move effectively, and position ourselves strategically. This preparation helps us make quick decisions, identify ways to escape, and select the right techniques when we encounter similar situations in the real world.

Outside of Krav Maga:

Public Speaking: In public speaking, visualization can boost your decision-making skills. Just imagine yourself in various situations, like handling tough questions or staying calm when there are technical issues. Repeatedly picturing these scenarios builds confidence and grace, helping you make the right choices during your actual presentation.

Negotiation: In the world of business negotiations, visualization exercises can be a game-changer. When you take the time to delve into different negotiation scenarios in your mind, ponder different offers and anticipate objections, you become better equipped to make smart strategic choices. This mental preparation boosts your ability to handle unexpected challenges and improves your chances of achieving favorable results.

Emergency Preparedness: In times of emergencies like fire drills or natural disasters, you can improve your decision-making skills by using visualization techniques. By imagining these situations in your mind, you can practice how to evacuate, evaluate risks, and plan the best responses. This mental rehearsal helps you make fast and effective decisions when faced with real emergencies, potentially saving lives and reducing damages.

Sports Performance: Athletes use visualization to make better decisions while playing. In soccer, for instance, they imagine different offensive and defensive situations, thinking about passes, shots, and strategies. By repeatedly imagining these scenarios, they improve their awareness, decision-making speed, and overall performance in real games.

Visualization is a powerful tool for improving decision-making skills. By mentally rehearsing different scenarios and exploring different responses, you gain a deeper understanding of the situations you may encounter. This preparation helps you make informed decisions, adapt quickly, and respond effectively, whether in Krav Maga or other areas of your life.

The benefits of enhanced focus go beyond just Krav Maga training. Visualization positively impacts various aspects of your life. It allows you to stay fully present and attentive in all situations, enhancing awareness, resilience, and adaptability.

Using visualization to strengthen the mind-body connection helps you navigate life's challenges with unwavering focus and concentration. It empowers you to tap into your full potential as a warrior, capable of responding to threats and adversities with a sharp and resolute mind.

Conclusion

Visualization is not just something Krav Maga practitioners do in their minds. It's a way of life for them. By using vivid mental rehearsals, they build their self-belief. This helps them face fear, handle stress, and make good decisions when things get tough. This practice goes beyond physical techniques. It creates a deep connection between the mind and body, giving them the strength to tackle life's challenges with courage and determination. Visualization is always with them, guiding their personal growth and inner strength. It makes every step of their Krav Maga journey more meaningful and transformative. With visualization as their ally, they embrace their inner warrior and go on a lifelong quest to overcome limits, conquer fears, and live with the unwavering spirit of a true Krav Maga warrior.

CHAPTER 15

Empathy

"Empathy's profound impact ripples through every aspect of life, nurturing empathy enriches personal connections and lays the groundwork for a more harmonious and compassionate world."

GM Dr. Neil Farber

In this chapter we discuss the pivotal role of empathy in your Krav Maga journey. Empathy is more than just a skill; it is a powerful tool that enhances your understanding of others and deepens your self-awareness, leading to a more profound and transformative experience in Krav Maga.

The Role of Empathy in Krav Maga

Empathy is a crucial value in the world of Krav Maga, influencing how you interact with each other and enhancing your training. This applies to various aspects of training, including partner drills and dynamic sparring sessions.

> *"At the heart of Krav Maga lies not just the skill to defend, but the empathy to understand; recognizing that true strength is as much about compassion as it is about combat."*

In partner drills, empathy plays a role when you take turns as attackers and defenders. By stepping into the shoes of the attacker, you develop an understanding of your training partner's vulnerabilities and fears. This understanding helps you effectively challenge your partner without overwhelming them emotionally or physically. It builds trust and creates a supportive environment where both participants can grow and learn together.

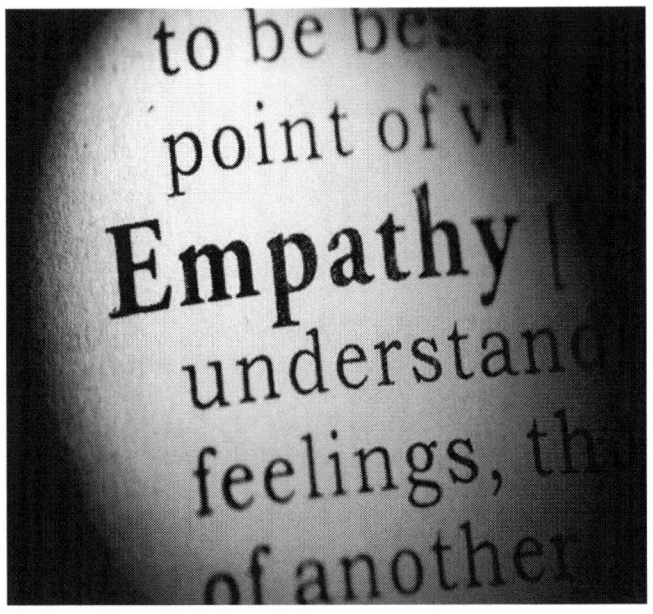

In dynamic sparring sessions, empathy allows you to be mindful of your partner's well-being. By controlling the intensity of strikes and using appropriate force, you ensure a safe and mutually beneficial experience. This empathetic approach fosters respect and camaraderie among training partners, encouraging you to push your limits and learn without fear of judgment or injury.

Empathy is crucial for teachers in creating a caring learning environment. They understand that each student comes to Krav Maga with different backgrounds, goals, and difficulties. Empathetic instructors adjust their teaching methods to meet individual needs, providing personalized guidance and support.

They also acknowledge that some students may have experienced past traumas or fears that affect their training. Empathetic instructors create a safe space for addressing these challenges, offering patience and encouragement to develop both physical skills and mental resilience.

In the context of self-defense scenarios, Krav Maga training often involves simulating high-stress situations. Empathy is important as students learn to understand the emotions and motivations of potential attackers or individuals in danger. This understanding helps students respond more effectively during simulations, leading to better decision-making in critical moments.

Empathy goes beyond just the physical. It also involves understanding and connecting with others on an emotional and psychological level. In the practice of Krav Maga, there are moments of frustration and self-doubt. But by practicing self-empathy and self-compassion, you can embrace the learning process and overcome setbacks, which leads to personal growth and resilience.

A key aspect of Krav Maga is empathy. It creates a supportive and respectful environment, enhances the effectiveness of self-defense techniques, and fosters personal development. By cultivating empathy with training partners, instructors, and oneself, you build a sense of unity and compassion within the Krav Maga community.

Empathy and Conflict Resolution

By developing and honing your empathetic skills, you can greatly improve your ability to handle conflicts in a more effective manner. This, in turn, creates a training environment that is more harmonious and supportive.

Empathy involves actively listening and genuinely trying to understand the perspectives and emotions of others. When conflicts arise, it is important to take the time to attentively listen to your training partners or opponents. This shows them respect and empathy for their experiences.

By making an effort to comprehend the underlying motivations and emotions behind their actions, you gain valuable insights into why conflicts occur. This understanding forms the foundation for constructive dialogue and resolution.

Krav Maga teaches you how to de-escalate potentially volatile situations using empathy as its central concept. Rather than impulsively reacting to aggression or conflict, you learn to approach adversaries with a compassionate and understanding mindset.

Understanding and acknowledging the feelings and concerns of others is key to effective communication. In order to defuse tension and promote peaceful resolution, it is important to approach conflicts with empathy and a genuine desire for understanding. Krav Maga, for example, is not about winning fights, but about ensuring your safety and that of your loved ones.

By empathizing with others, you can find common ground and shared goals, which can help bridge the gap between conflicting parties. This sense of unity can transform adversaries into potential allies, fostering collaboration and problem-solving.

Moreover, empathy plays a crucial role in regulating emotions during conflicts. By recognizing and empathizing with the emotions of others, as well as understanding your own emotional responses, you can approach conflicts with a calm and composed demeanor. This emotional regulation enhances your ability to think clearly and make level-headed decisions, preventing conflicts from escalating into volatile situations.

In summary, empathy is a powerful tool for effective communication and conflict resolution. It allows for the discovery of shared interests, promotes unity and collaboration, and helps maintain emotional stability during tense moments. By practicing empathy, we can work towards resolutions that benefit everyone involved.

Empathy Beyond the Training Mat

As you train and become more empathetic, you begin to notice and understand the emotions and experiences of others in your everyday life. This empathy becomes a guiding force in how you interact with your family, friends, and colleagues. It helps you to be compassionate, kind, and understanding, and overall, a more emotionally intelligent person. Embracing empathy allows you to make a positive impact not only within your Krav Maga community but also in the world at large. It enriches your relationships, deepens your connections with others, and creates a safe and supportive environment for open communication. By understanding and empathizing with others, you build trust and foster more fulfilling relationships.

Empathy fosters a sense of community and support both within and outside the Krav Maga training environment. By empathizing with the challenges and triumphs of your training partners and peers, you contribute to a culture of camaraderie and encouragement.

Empathy goes beyond just being understanding on the training mat. It can actually help you create supportive communities in different social settings. Instead of jumping to conclusions in conflicts, empathy allows you to approach them with patience and an open mind. It helps you understand other people's perspectives and leads to better resolutions.

> *"Empathy, the silent lesson of Krav Maga, enriches our life tapestry; infusing our choices with kindness, our relationships with depth, and our journey with a profound sense of purpose."*

Empathy isn't limited to borders or cultures. It gives you a global perspective and helps you appreciate diversity. By empathizing with people from different backgrounds, you become more connected to humanity and are more likely to help out in your community. Empathy breaks down cultural barriers and makes the world feel like one big community.

When you embrace empathy in your interactions with people from all walks of life, you contribute to a more compassionate and inclusive world. Empathy becomes a force that brings people together and helps everyone understand each other's experiences.

It is said that there are 3 types of empathy: *Physical*, *Emotional* and *Intuitive*. "Empaths" tend to be sensitive, loving, have big hearts with finely tuned intuition. Becoming a full-blooded "empath" is not what I'm suggesting, but being truly empathetic has fantastic positive consequences.

Physical: Being attuned to other people's physical symptoms. People that are "overly empathic" may tend to absorb these symptoms into their bodies – not in a healthy way.

Emotional: Picking up other people's emotions and being a sponge for their feelings.

Intuitive: Experiencing extraordinary perceptions such as heightened intuition. This helps sense and predict things thanks to gut feelings and powerful intuition.

By embracing empathy, conflicts transform into chances to evolve and comprehend, resulting in more fulfilled relationships and a kinder way of resolving differences. When you embrace empathy in your Krav Maga practice, it improves your ability to engage in productive communication and find resolutions for conflicts in all areas of life.

Conclusion

By practicing empathy, you can understand others and ourselves better, forming stronger connections in the Krav Maga community and throughout life. Empathy helps you de-escalate conflicts, find common ground, and approach difficult situations with compassion and wisdom. It improves your relationships and creates supportive communities that promote growth and unity. Empathy becomes a valuable tool for navigating conflicts and turning them into opportunities for understanding and resolution. By embracing empathy, you can see the world in a more inclusive and compassionate way, spreading empathy on a global scale.

Incorporating empathy into your Krav Maga practice not only improves your self-defense skills but also nurtures your ability to be empathetic, understanding, and patient individuals. As you embrace empathy, realize its profound impact on shaping a more harmonious and connected world. Every interaction becomes a chance to bring about positive change through compassion and understanding.

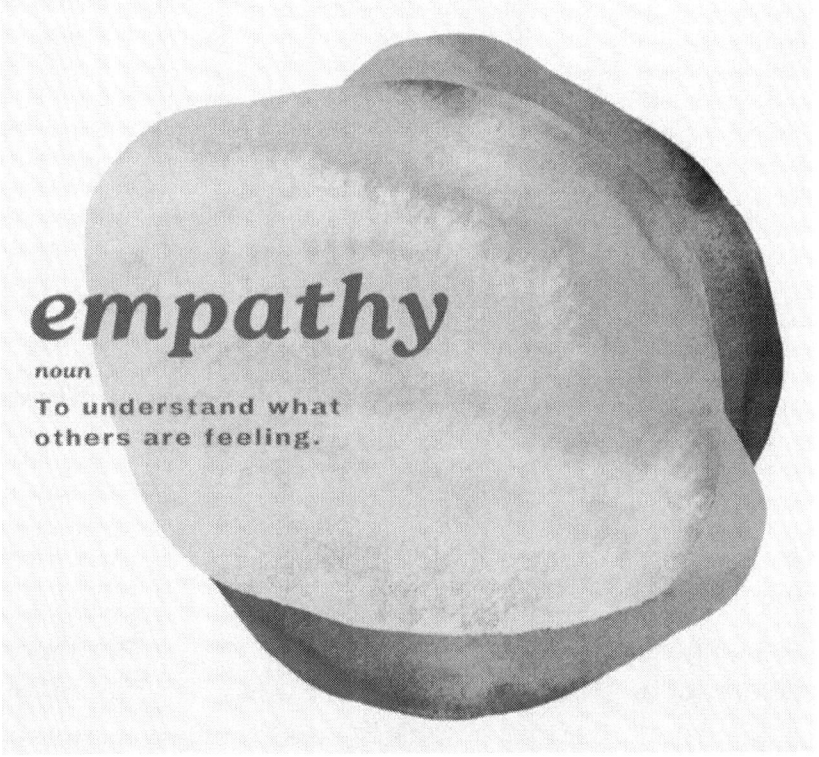

CHAPTER 16

Emotional Regulation

"Emotional regulation in Krav Maga is more than keeping composure; it's channeling every emotion—fear, anger, passion—into purposeful movement, turning inner storms into strategic winds."

Dr. GM Neil Farber

In this chapter we explore the concept of emotional regulation. How it relates and is cultivated in Krav Maga and how it becomes a transformative practice empowering you to manage emotions effectively in both training and real-life situations.

Krav Maga and Emotional Regulation

In the world of Krav Maga training, intensity is intentionally dialed up to replicate high-stress situations. This unique approach aims to equip you with the necessary skills and mindset to handle real-life encounters. Engaging in such rigorous training can evoke a wide range of emotions, including fear, frustration, and anxiety. However, instead of shying away from these feelings, you're encouraged to confront and process them within a safe and supportive environment.

By directly facing your emotions, you become better equipped at regulating your emotional responses. This newfound ability allows you to stay focused and make rational decisions even when under immense pressure.

One of the key teachings of Krav Maga is the art of channeling emotions into productive and purpose-driven actions. Rather than being overwhelmed by fear or anger, you're taught to leverage these emotions as sources of determination and resolve. In essence, Krav Maga empowers you to transform your emotions into powerful forces that propel you forward instead of holding you back.

Harnessing your emotions can help you perform at your best, especially in self-defense situations where quick thinking is crucial. Through Krav Maga training, you learn to face and conquer physical and mental challenges, building emotional resilience. This resilience extends beyond the training, empowering you to handle stress and difficult situations in your everyday life. By regulating your emotions and staying composed, you will develop inner strength and adaptability, allowing you to navigate life's obstacles with grace and determination.

> *"Krav Maga isn't merely a practice of defense; it's a deep dive into the art of emotional regulation, transforming raw reactions into mindful, masterful actions."*

By cultivating present-moment awareness during training, you learn to observe your emotions without judgment. This mindfulness in movement allows you to recognize the signs of emotional arousal and respond thoughtfully rather than react impulsively.

Krav Maga has a deep connection to emotional regulation. When you embrace the intensity of Krav Maga training, you learn to channel your emotions into productive action. This practice cultivates resilience and teaches you how to be mindful in your movements.

The Krav Mind goes far beyond physical self-defense. It transforms you into a person who is emotionally intelligent and composed in all aspects of life. By regulating your emotions effectively, you gain the power to confront challenges with a steady and focused mindset. This emotional resilience and inner strength will help you navigate life's complexities with confidence.

Techniques for Emotional Regulation in Krav Maga

One of the fundamental techniques for emotional regulation in Krav Maga involves focused breathing exercises and centering techniques. By consciously regulating your breath, you can calm your nervous system and regain control over your emotional state.

One of the key ways to regulate emotions in Krav Maga is through focused breathing and centering techniques. By consciously controlling your breath, you can calm your nervous system and regain control over your emotions.

> *"Krav Maga teaches us that the arena of self-defense is as much about emotional landscapes as physical confrontations. Emotional regulation is the foundation, guiding each move with clarity and precision."*

In high-stress or emotionally intense situations, you practice deep, rhythmic breathing. This simple but powerful technique helps reduce stress and focus your mind, leading to emotional stability and better decision-making.

Another helpful tool is visualization, as we've discussed. By mentally rehearsing scenarios where you conquer challenging emotions, you build resilience. Visualization allows you to identify and process emotional triggers, practicing your responses in a controlled mental space. This empowers you to approach real-life situations with emotional preparedness, allowing you to remain composed and regulate your emotions effectively.

Krav Maga helps you regulate your emotions by gradually exposing you to challenging situations. This technique, called progressive desensitization, builds your resilience, and teaches you to manage your emotions effectively. After intense training, you reflect on your emotional experiences and discuss them with others. By openly communicating your feelings, you gain insights from your peers and instructor, and improve your ability to regulate emotions in both training and real-life situations. Developing your emotional regulation skills through Krav Maga enhances your self-awareness and overall well-being, boosting your chances of success in all aspects of life.

Emotional Resilience Beyond Krav Maga

By learning to control your emotions and stay calm during intense training sessions, you develop the ability to handle life's challenges better. When you face stressful situations at work, in relationships, or in other areas of life, you can use your emotional resilience to stay focused and clear-headed.

This resilience helps you approach problems with a balanced mindset and gives you a sense of control and adaptability. Krav Maga's focus on emotional regulation prepares you to deal with tough times and setbacks more effectively. By facing and overcoming challenges during training, you gain confidence in your ability to handle difficult situations. This belief in your resilience extends beyond the training mat, inspiring you to confront obstacles in life with determination and perseverance. Emotional resilience allows you to bounce back from setbacks, learn from failures, and keep moving forward with a positive and growth-oriented attitude.

> *"Krav Maga instills a mastery of emotional regulation, transforming how we navigate the myriad battles of everyday life with grace and insight."*

Emotional resilience plays a significant role in enhancing your interpersonal relationships. By managing your emotions and staying composed during conflicts, you can engage in more constructive and empathetic communication.

Mastering emotional regulation is the key to better relationships and success in high-pressure environments.

Whether it's dealing with family, friends, or colleagues, being able to navigate through emotionally charged situations with grace and self-control is essential. It allows for active listening, empathy, and a genuine desire to understand others, leading to more meaningful and harmonious connections.

In professional or academic settings where the heat is turned up, emotional resilience becomes even more crucial. The ability to remain calm and focused during stressful situations is what sets you apart from the competition and allows you to thrive in challenging environments.

Krav Maga, with its emphasis on emotional resilience, equips you with the tools necessary to tackle deadlines, presentations, or exams with confidence and adaptability. By managing stress and emotions under pressure, you enhance your performance and increase your chances of achieving success in any endeavor you undertake.

The power of emotional resilience affects every aspect of your life. By learning how to manage stress, overcome difficult situations, and build strong relationships, you tap into a whole new level of emotional control. This newfound resilience doesn't just change you personally; it also has an impact on your professional life. You'll be able to face challenges with confidence, empathy, and a sense of inner strength. Through nurturing your emotional resilience, you'll embark on a journey of self-improvement and well-being, becoming a true warrior who handles life's ups and downs with grace. And along the way, you'll inspire others and make a positive difference in the world.

Emotional Regulation and Emotional Intelligence

Emotional regulation and emotional intelligence are connected in the world of Krav Maga. Emotional intelligence

(EI) involves recognizing and managing one's own emotions, as well as understanding and empathizing with others. EI has been shown in research studies to be more predictive of success in business, than is IQ. Krav Maga helps develop emotional intelligence through training.

By practicing emotional regulation techniques, you become more in tune with your emotions and learn to control them effectively. This self-awareness is a key part of emotional intelligence.

In Krav Maga, you also practice empathy and social skills by working with training partners and instructors. The supportive training environment helps build effective communication, conflict resolution, and teamwork, which are all crucial aspects of emotional intelligence. In Krav Maga, you also practice empathy and social skills by engaging with training partners and instructors.

> *"In the heart of Krav Maga lies a lesson not just of self-defense, but of emotional intelligence: to truly defend, one must first understand both self and adversary."*

The cooperative and respectful nature of the training environment fosters the development of effective communication, conflict resolution, and teamwork—essential aspects of emotional intelligence.

In your personal life, emotional intelligence is key to how your interact and engage with others. By practicing Krav Maga, you can enhance your emotional intelligence, which helps you better understand and connect with the feelings of those around you. This understanding allows you to respond to others with kindness and sensitivity, making them feel acknowledged and heard in your presence.

When you learn to regulate your emotions, you become adept at handling conflicts in a positive way. Instead of reacting impulsively, you approach disagreements with a calm and composed attitude, aiming for resolution and understanding rather than making things worse. Your ability to navigate conflicts with maturity and emotional intelligence promotes open communication and positive outcomes, establishing trust and respect in your relationships.

Conclusion

In this chapter, we've learned that emotional regulation is not just a side skill but a crucial part of becoming a true Krav Maga warrior. By incorporating techniques to control your emotions into your training, you go on a journey of self-awareness and personal growth. Through breathing exercises, visualization, progressive desensitization, and reflective practices, you gain a variety of tools to effectively manage your emotions. These techniques empower you to stay calm during high-pressure situations, make rational decisions, and have a deep understanding of yourself.

KRAV MIND

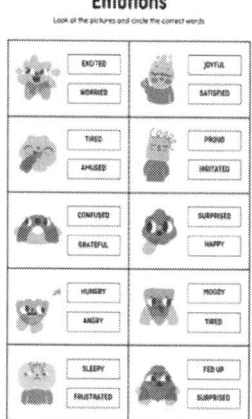

Developing emotional intelligence is a natural result of practicing emotional regulation in Krav Maga. As you become more aware of your own emotions, you also become sensitive to the emotions of others. This heightened empathy and social awareness allow you to handle personal relationships with better understanding, cooperation, and compassion.

These techniques enable you to stay composed during high-stress scenarios, make rational decisions, and cultivate a profound sense of self-awareness.

Emotional intelligence emerges as a natural extension of emotional regulation in Krav Maga. As you develop a deeper understanding of your emotions, you also become attuned to the emotions of others. This heightened empathy and social awareness allow you to navigate personal relationships with greater understanding, cooperation, and compassion.

By practicing Krav Maga, you can develop emotional intelligence and become a well-rounded individual. Not only will you become skilled in self-defense, but you will also learn how to be resilient and empathetic in all areas of your life.

The lessons you learn in Krav Maga will extend beyond the training environment and improve your interactions, relationships, and overall well-being.

When you incorporate emotional intelligence into your daily life, you create a positive social environment where conflicts are handled well, and connections deepen. You will become a beacon of emotional awareness, positively impacting yourself and those around you.

Krav Maga empowers you to unleash your hidden potential as a warrior, equipped not only with self-defense skills but also with emotional mastery. It will foster personal growth and enhance the world with compassion and empathy.

CHAPTER 17

Gratitude

"Gratitude is the heart's armor in Krav Maga, as it reminds us of the lessons learned, the strength gained, and the community that empowers us to face life's challenges with courage and appreciation."

GM Dr. Neil Farber

In this chapter, we investigate the power of gratitude within the realm of Krav Maga and beyond. Discover how Krav Maga cultivates gratitude, learn to express it in everyday life, and explore its profound impact on mental well-being.

The Power of Gratitude

Gratitude is a powerful emotion that can transform your life. It's more than just saying "thank you" - it's about appreciating all the good things in your life and the people who enrich it. Scientific research has proven that practicing gratitude can have a profound impact on your mental, emotional, and physical well-being.

Studies show that regularly cultivating gratitude leads to increased happiness, contentment, and life satisfaction. It also reduces stress levels, improves sleep quality, and enhances overall mental health. Gratitude acts as a shield against depression and anxiety, helping you bounce back from challenges.

> *"The power of gratitude is transformative. It turns what we have into enough, challenges into lessons, and everyday moments into extraordinary memories."*

When you focus on the good things in your life and express gratitude for them, your perspective changes. Instead of thinking about what you don't have, you start to appreciate  what you do. This way of thinking brings a feeling of abundance and satisfaction, which helps you stop feeling jealous or comparing yourself to others. You become more present in the moment and you enjoy and value the blessings and happiness that are already part of your life.

Being grateful is not only good for you individually, but also for your relationships and communities. When you show gratitude to others, it strengthens your connections with them, deepens your bonds, and helps you feel like you belong. Being grateful creates a cycle of positivity, where acts of appreciation and kindness are returned, making you even happier and more connected.

In the world of Krav Maga, gratitude becomes even more meaningful. When you go through tough training, you face challenges that require you to be resilient and determined. Through this journey, you learn to be thankful for your body's abilities, your mental strength, and the support of your training partners and instructors. Embracing gratitude in Krav Maga training helps you find motivation in difficulties, seeing them as opportunities to improve instead of setbacks.

Incorporating gratitude into your Krav Maga, can have a profound impact on your life. Gratitude has the incredible power to change how you see the world, allowing you to appreciate the beauty and goodness in everything - both in yourself and in the world around you. As you approach life with a grateful heart, you'll unlock a whole new realm of possibilities and find a deeper sense of purpose and fulfillment.

How Krav Maga Helps You Develop Gratitude

Krav Maga training is a powerful tool for developing resilience and mental strength. The tough and demanding nature of the training pushes you to your limits, both physically and mentally. By facing challenging techniques and demanding drills, you learn to overcome obstacles and persevere through tough times. This journey of growth and progress creates an environment where gratitude naturally flourishes.

> *"Every session in Krav Maga becomes a testament to gratitude. Through each strike and defense, we discover the gift of our capacities, the value of camaraderie, and the profound lessons hidden in challenges."*

Through the ups and downs of Krav Maga, you learn to be grateful for every experience. Even in the face of difficulties, you appreciate the chance to grow and improve. Each time you step onto the training mat, you're grateful for your body's abilities, the support of your training partners, and the guidance of your instructors. Embracing gratitude as a mindset helps you see setbacks as opportunities and find lessons in every situation.

As anyone who practices Krav Maga knows, accidents and injuries are likely to occur. After training for many years and experiencing some painful injuries, you truly appreciate good health and the ability to function normally. Even a minor injury can bring feelings of gratitude that it wasn't something more serious.

As you dive into the world of Krav Maga, gratitude becomes a crucial part of your training and everyday life. Showing appreciation for your skills, progress, and the efforts of others strengthens a positive and empowering mindset. Gratitude influences how you interact with your training partners, instructors, and the whole Krav Maga community, creating a supportive and encouraging atmosphere.

Krav Maga goes beyond physical techniques and helps you develop gratitude for the entire journey. Each training session serves as an opportunity to practice self-compassion, patience, and determination. By embracing 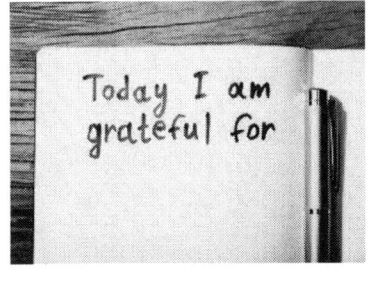 gratitude, you shift your focus from seeking perfection to celebrating progress, no matter how small. This mindset of appreciating the journey keeps you motivated and committed, transforming Krav Maga into a fulfilling and life-changing experience.

As you practice Krav Maga and cultivate gratitude, you start to see the world differently. Gratitude becomes like a pair of glasses that helps you appreciate even the little things in life. It helps you enjoy the present, connect better with people, and find beauty in everyday moments. When you fully embrace gratitude in your Krav Maga practice, it empowers you to live a life filled with appreciation, resilience, and personal growth.

Expressing Gratitude in Everyday Life

Gratitude goes beyond mere emotion- it has the power to manifest in our actions. By incorporating gratitude into your Krav Maga practice, you can extend this positive mindset to all areas of your life.

Taking a moment to acknowledge and value your own efforts, accomplishments, and growth in Krav Maga and beyond is an essential component of self-compassion and self-care. Celebrating even the smallest victories and recognizing that each progress demonstrates your commitment and strength will help build a solid foundation of self-esteem and a positive self-perception.

Gratitude is a powerful force that not only strengthens relationships and creates a sense of community, but also can transform your personal growth and outlook on life. In the world of Krav Maga, expressing appreciation to your training partners and instructors helps foster a supportive and uplifting environment. By acknowledging the contributions of others in both your training and daily lives, establishes connections and a sense of belonging. Even simple acts of gratitude, like saying "thank you" or giving a genuine compliment, can make a significant impact on others and set off a positive chain reaction.

Utilizing gratitude as a tool for personal growth and self-improvement allows you to shift your perspective when faced with challenges. Rather than dwelling on negativity during setbacks or obstacles, you can look for lessons and opportunities for growth. By embracing gratitude as a catalyst for learning and resilience, you can bounce back stronger from adversity. Seeing challenges as a chance to learn and develop enables you to transform difficulties into stepping stones that propel you closer to your goals.

Additionally, expressing gratitude can enhance your overall well-being and mental health. Research has shown that regularly practicing gratitude can lead to increased feelings of happiness, reduced stress levels, and improved overall life satisfaction. Gratitude serves as a buffer against negative emotions, fostering a positive outlook even in challenging circumstances.

> *"Krav Maga is more than a martial art; it's a celebration of gratitude. In every move, we're reminded of life's fragility, our innate power, and the infinite gifts embedded in the present moment."*

Incorporating gratitude into your daily routine doesn't have to be complicated. Keeping a gratitude journal, where you write down things, you're thankful for each day, can have a big impact. It helps you stay positive and grateful. Taking a moment to thank someone who has made a difference in your life, whether through a heartfelt note or a small gesture, can strengthen your relationships and make you feel more connected.

As you make gratitude a regular part of your life, you'll find that it naturally becomes a powerful mindset. By expressing gratitude to yourself and others, you'll cultivate a positive outlook that improves your well-being, strengthens your relationships, and helps you grow as a person. Embrace gratitude as a guiding force in your journey of self-improvement, and let it enrich every aspect of your life, from your workouts to your interactions with others, and the way you approach challenges and opportunities.

Gratitude and Mental Well-Being

The act of being grateful has a huge impact on your mental well-being. It helps you regulate your emotions, reduces stress, and improves your overall psychological health. By practicing gratitude in your Krav Maga journey and everyday life, you will realize how powerful it can be for your mental health.

Gratitude plays an important role in helping you manage and navigate through a wide range of emotions. When you focus on the positive aspects of your experiences and express your thankfulness, it changes your perspective. This shift in perspective helps you handle negative emotions more effectively, bringing a sense of balance and stability to your emotional state. Gratitude also allows you to find comfort during difficult times and approach challenges with a more positive and constructive mindset.

Incorporating gratitude practices into your daily life can also reduce stress and anxiety. By actively recognizing and appreciating the positive things in your life, you are less likely to dwell on negative thoughts or worries. When you redirect your attention to what you are grateful for, it helps alleviate stress and anxiety, creating a more tranquil and peaceful state of mind.

Adding gratitude to your self-care routine is a great way to improve your mental well-being. By taking a moment to appreciate and be thankful for your efforts, accomplishments, and growth, you strengthen a positive image of yourself and boost your self-esteem. Being grateful for yourself also boosts your self-confidence and helps you be kinder to yourself, which are important for mental resilience and well-being.

> *"Krav Maga teaches us to be warriors, not just in combat but in life. This gratitude for every lesson, every challenge, enriches our mental well-being, making us resilient, hopeful, and deeply connected."*

As you make gratitude a habit, you'll notice that it works well with other self-care practices like mindfulness and relaxation techniques. Gratitude keeps you grounded and helps you stay focused on the positive aspects of your life. It's especially helpful during tough times, giving you strength and optimism as you face challenges.

Research has proven that regularly practicing gratitude has numerous mental health benefits. This includes feeling happier, having fewer symptoms of depression, and being more satisfied with life overall. Gratitude also helps you feel more connected to others and encourages you to act in ways that benefit your social life.

As you begin your journey of incorporating gratitude into your life, keep in mind that it is a skill that can be developed over time. By consciously recognizing and expressing gratitude for the good things in your life, you will improve your mental well-being and be better equipped to handle challenges. Embrace the life-changing power of gratitude, and let it guide you toward a stronger mind, a healthier emotional state, and a more meaningful life, both in and out of your everyday experience.

Conclusion

This chapter illuminated the transformative power of gratitude in enhancing your mental well-being. By acknowledging and being thankful for the good things in your life, you can build emotional strength, reduce stress, and feel more connected to others. Practicing gratitude through the martial art of Krav Maga can be especially impactful, as the challenges and victories it brings can teach you to appreciate growth and progress. By embracing gratitude in your daily life, you can empower yourself to live a more meaningful and emotionally fulfilling life. Let gratitude guide you on your journey to better mental health and self-discovery, and watch as it adds richness to every aspect of your life.

CHAPTER 18

Leadership

"A martial arts leader's legacy is not etched in stone, but carved in the hearts of those they have guided to greatness."

Dr. GM Neil Farber

In this chapter, we look closely at the profound influence of leadership in Krav Maga. It goes beyond just having a position of authority - involves important qualities that motivate, assist, and empower the whole community. As we examine the key traits of successful leaders and how they shape the training atmosphere, we also uncover how these qualities enhance every aspects of life outside martial arts.

Defining Leadership: Traits and Qualities

Leadership in Krav Maga involves more than just having power or authority. It is about inspiring and guiding others towards a shared goal, promoting growth, and making a positive impact on individuals and communities. A leader in Krav Maga must possess certain traits and qualities.

Vision and Purpose: Effective leadership is all about having a clear vision and purpose. In the world of Krav Maga, leaders have a strong and motivating vision for personal growth and the development of their fellow practitioners. They imagine a supportive community, where everyone can flourish, enhance their abilities, and feel confident in tackling challenges both in and out of training. This powerful vision guides their choices and actions, paving the way for continual progress and achievement.

Self-Confidence and Empathy: Confidence is crucial for leaders in Krav Maga. However, it is important to clarify that this confidence is not rooted in arrogance, but rather comes from a deep understanding of one's own abilities and a belief in the potential of others. Leaders in this discipline inspire confidence in their training partners, boosting their morale and helping them surpass their own limitations.

Equally significant is the trait of empathy. Effective leaders in Krav Maga take the time to understand the unique challenges and aspirations of each individual under their guidance. This understanding enables them to offer personalized support and guidance. By empathizing with the struggles and successes of their peers, leaders create an environment that is inclusive and compassionate, where everyone feels appreciated and respected.

Integrity and Accountability: Integrity is vital for leaders in all situations, including Krav Maga. These leaders embrace honesty, transparency, and ethical behavior, serving as a model for others. They prioritize fairness, humility, and responsible choices, holding themselves responsible for their actions and creating a benchmark for others to emulate.

Effective Communication: In Krav Maga, good leadership hinges on strong communication skills. Leaders must be able to express their vision clearly, offer helpful feedback, and encourage open and honest conversations among participants. By communicating effectively, leaders foster a sense of unity and ensure that everyone is working towards common objectives. While many see leaders as those who confidently speak up, true leadership also involves being willing to sit down and actively listen to others; it's all about two-way communication.

Adaptability and Resilience: In the dynamic and challenging environment of Krav Maga, leaders need to be adaptable and resilient. They must embrace change and find creative solutions when faced with obstacles. By showing resilience in the face of setbacks, leaders inspire their training partners to keep going and stay determined.

Mentorship and Growth Mindset: Leaders in Krav Maga act as mentors, guiding and supporting others on their martial arts journey. These leaders are focused on fostering a growth mindset, encouraging a continuous desire to learn and improve. By creating a culture of learning and development, they empower practitioners to overcome their fears and evolve both physically and mentally.

Leadership in Krav Maga is not about having authority or dominating others. Instead, it is about serving as a catalyst for growth and unity. Effective leaders embody a vision of progress and empowerment. They lead by example, setting the standards for others to follow. They also foster a culture of respect and support within the community.

To be a leader in Krav Maga, one must possess certain qualities. These include self-confidence, empathy, integrity, effective communication, adaptability, and resilience. By embodying these traits, leaders inspire and elevate the entire community. They create a positive and transformative experience for all practitioners.

> *"To lead is to serve with heart and vision, recognizing that the true measure of leadership is not just in milestones achieved, but in the lives touched, inspired, and uplifted along the way."*

Becoming a leader in Krav Maga is not an endpoint but an ongoing process of self-discovery and personal growth. It also paves the way for enhancing leadership qualities in all aspects of life beyond the training mat.

Leadership in Krav Maga: Nurturing Effective Instructors

Krav Maga helps people become great leaders and teachers in their community. By teaching principles like responsibility, discipline, and empathy, Krav Maga nurtures the qualities needed to guide and mentor others on their own journey of personal development. Let's discover how Krav Maga develops leadership skills and transforms its practitioners into inspiring instructors who can share their knowledge and empower others.

> *"Being a leader is not about shining in the spotlight, but illuminating the way for others, ensuring their path is clear, their potential recognized, and their aspirations within reach."*

Leading by Example: In Krav Maga, being a leader is more than just teaching and giving orders. It's about setting a good example and showing others how to embody the core values of Krav Maga. Effective leaders in Krav Maga live by integrity, discipline, and humility, both in and out of training. By practicing what they teach, they gain the trust and respect of their students, creating a positive learning environment. They know that actions speak louder than words and strive to be proof of how Krav Maga can transform lives.

Leading by example also means being resilient and determined, even in the face of setbacks. It requires a mindset of continuous growth and humility, as there is always more to learn and improve upon. Krav Maga leaders approach each training session with an open mind, seeking new knowledge and refining their techniques. This commitment to personal growth inspires others to do the same, fostering a culture of support and encouragement.

Additionally, leading by example involves creating a supportive training environment. Leaders in Krav Maga actively engage with their training partners, providing helpful feedback and encouragement.

They understand and respect the limits of others, making sure that everyone feels valued and safe during training. They promote teamwork and camaraderie, working together to overcome challenges and improve their skills as a group.

Experienced practitioners and instructors are fully dedicated to their training. They work hard to improve their skills and techniques, both physically and mentally. They understand the importance of balance and discipline in personal growth. By showing their commitment and focus, they motivate others to take their training seriously. This is particularly important when it comes to welcoming newbies and nurturing talent. Experienced practitioners cheer on their fellow practitioners, creating an environment of support and celebration. They invest in the growth and development of others, fostering a positive and motivating atmosphere that inspires everyone to reach their fullest potential.

Empowering Others to Excel: Leadership in Krav Maga is all about empowering others to excel and reach their full potential by being mentors. Instructors guide students through challenges, setbacks, and triumphs, recognizing that each student is on their own unique journey and tailor their guidance and instruction accordingly. This creates an inclusive and supportive environment. Leaders understand that everyone learns at their own pace and adapt their teaching methods to meet individual needs; no one is left behind. Empowering others through mentorship not only enhances the learning experience but also strengthens the sense of community within Krav Maga.

Communicating with Clarity and Compassion: To be a great leader, you must communicate clearly and with kindness. In Krav Maga, instructors excel at teaching difficult moves and ideas in a way that connects with their students. They remove any barriers and make the training fun for everyone. Krav Maga leaders listen carefully to their students' questions and worries, offering helpful advice and support with understanding and respect. This creates a strong bond between the students and instructors, allowing students to feel at ease seeking guidance and sharing their thoughts.

Emphasizing Growth Mindset: The leaders of Krav Maga believe in the power of continuous learning. They teach their students to see challenges and mistakes as chances to grow and get better. They remind them that setbacks are not signs of failure but important steps on the path to success. Creating a positive and growth-focused environment, these leaders motivate their students to keep going, adapt, and aim for excellence in everything they do.

Leading Beyond the Mat: Leadership skills developed in Krav Maga extend far beyond the training mat. Practitioners become influential figures in their communities, empowering others to navigate life's challenges with resilience and determination. The qualities honed through Krav Maga, such as self-discipline, problem-solving, and emotional intelligence, enable leaders to excel in various domains, from their professional careers to personal relationships.

Krav Maga's profound impact on leadership shapes individuals into empathetic, inspiring, and compassionate instructors. By leading by example, empowering others, communicating effectively, embracing growth, and applying leadership skills beyond the training mat, Krav Maga leaders uplift their communities and leave an enduring legacy of transformation and empowerment.

Transferable Leadership Skills Applying Leadership Beyond Krav Maga

The leadership skills gained from Krav Maga training have a profound impact on different areas of people's lives. I will examine how these valuable lessons can be used in professional settings, personal relationships, and community involvement. By doing so, I will demonstrate how Krav Maga's leadership development has real-world benefits beyond the training mat.

Effective Communication and Conflict Resolution: Krav Maga leaders are great at communicating and resolving conflicts. These skills are useful in both work and personal life. In the workplace, good communication helps teams work together and understand each other better. You can use your conflict resolution abilities to handle disagreements calmly and diplomatically, which leads to better outcomes. In personal relationships, you can resolve arguments with kindness and understanding, keeping the interaction healthy and positive. In a professional setting, you can use your communication skills to listen to your colleagues during meetings and make sure everyone feels heard. When conflicts arise, you can address concerns calmly and find a solution that works for everyone.

Empowering and Mentoring Others: As a leader in Krav Maga, you have the ability to empower and mentor others to reach their full potential. This skill can be easily applied in a work environment, where you can guide and support your younger colleagues, helping them grow professionally. Additionally, you can also volunteer as a mentor in community programs, inspiring and guiding individuals to develop themselves and improve their lives. Furthermore, your expertise in empowering others in the gym can extend to your profession, where you can take on a junior colleague as a mentee. By offering them guidance, encouragement, and valuable insights, you can help them excel in their career.

Decision-Making Under Pressure: The skill to make quick and smart decisions when the pressure is on is what sets Krav Maga leaders apart. This ability is especially important in demanding industries or when important moments arise.

You have perfected your decision-making skills and can stay calm in tough situations, reducing risks and making confident choices. In a business environment, you calmly handle unexpected crises, swiftly evaluating the situation and putting in place a plan to minimize damage and get things back to normal as soon as possible.

Leading with Empathy and Emotional Intelligence: The best leaders in Krav Maga know that empathy and emotional intelligence are crucial for creating a positive and supportive atmosphere. These qualities also apply to your professional life, where you lead with compassion and understand the needs and goals of your team members. In personal relationships, you connect deeply with your loved ones, forming meaningful and fulfilling bonds. When you lead with empathy in the gym, it carries over to the workplace too. You recognize the emotions and concerns of your team during tough projects, offering emotional support and encouragement. This creates an environment where everyone feels valued and motivated to do their best.

Goal-Oriented and Resilient Mindset: Krav Maga cultivates a mindset focused on goals and resilience. This mentality extends beyond training and into all aspects of life. In professional endeavors, you set ambitious objectives and demonstrate determination in overcoming obstacles to achieve success. In personal pursuits, you embrace challenges with the mindset of constant improvement, always striving for personal growth. Applying the same determination and goal-setting in the gym, you also set fitness goals outside of training and work consistently towards achieving them through dedication and perseverance.

Conclusion

Leadership in Krav Maga goes beyond being a trainer or instructor. It involves important qualities and skills that apply to all areas of life. Krav Maga helps you become a good communicator, a mentor who empowers others, a confident decision-maker, a compassionate leader, and someone who sets goals and leads by example. These leadership skills are not confined to the training mat; they have a real impact in the real world. They enable you to inspire and motivate others, build strong relationships, and make a positive difference in your community. Embracing leadership in Krav Maga is about more than just improving yourself; it's about making a meaningful and lasting impact on the world.

CHAPTER 19

Empowerment

"In Krav Maga, empowerment begins with embracing your vulnerabilities and transforming them into sources of strength and resilience."

GM Dr. Neil Farber

Empowerment is a powerful concept that combines strength, independence, and self-discovery. I've previously discussed the many positive effects of Krav Maga on mental well-being. Now, let's imagine what a person who practices Krav Maga and possesses traits like accountability, resilience, empathy, confidence, mindfulness, discipline, and leadership would be like. The word that best describes them is "empowered". In this chapter, I will delve into the transformative power of Krav Maga and how it can empower you. I'll explore how practicing Krav Maga helps you uncover your inner strength and how this personal growth has a profound impact on the world around you.

Defining Empowerment

Empowerment has become a buzzword in recent years, celebrated in various areas from personal growth to business dynamics. Essentially, empowerment is about discovering and utilizing your inherent power and potential. It guides you in today's complex world, enabling you to be confident, make independent decisions, and create positive change in your surroundings.

> *"To be empowered is to wear courage as your armor and vision as your compass, navigating life's journey with unwavering determination."*

The concept of empowerment originated from social movements and academic circles, where marginalized groups and individuals sought recognition and influence. It represents gaining control over your life, choices, and environment. In personal development, empowerment goes beyond external control; it is primarily about self-mastery. This involves understanding yourself, acknowledging your strengths and weaknesses, and using this knowledge to navigate life's challenges

The term "empowerment" is frequently used in place of other similar terms. Let's compare it to a few related concepts:

- **Self-efficacy:** This refers to your belief in your ability to complete tasks and achieve goals. While self-efficacy focuses on believing in your capabilities, empowerment takes it a step further by encouraging you to use those capabilities in real-life situations.
- **Independence:** Independence means being self-sufficient and free from external control. Empowerment, however, goes beyond independence by combining it

with a sense of purpose, motivating you to create positive change in both personal and larger contexts.
- **Leadership:** Leadership is a term we hear a lot, both in professional and social settings. It involves guiding and inspiring others to achieve a common goal. It's about being in charge and making decisions to keep a team or group moving forward together. Leadership is about empowering others, but it's also about looking outward and mobilizing those around you. On the other hand, empowerment is broader in scope. It starts from within and focuses on personal growth, self-belief, and mastering oneself. An empowered person is independent, confident, and driven, regardless of their position of leadership. While all effective leaders may embody empowered qualities, not all empowered individuals necessarily take on traditional leadership roles.

Empowerment stands out because it combines self-belief, action, and influence in a unique way. In the world of Krav Maga, empowerment takes on an even greater significance. Krav Maga instills a mindset rooted in self-awareness and determination, closely aligned with the essence of empowerment, which we will explore further in the upcoming section.

Building blocks of empowerment

Accountability: Empowerment starts when you take responsibility for your actions and development in Krav Maga. By holding yourself accountable for your training and progress, you become actively involved in your journey towards empowerment. Recognizing your own strengths and weaknesses enables you to work on specific areas for self-improvement and strive for continuous excellence.

Resilience: Developing resilience is crucial in mastering Krav Maga. By subjecting yourself to rigorous training situations, you acquire the ability to recover from hardships, adjust to unexpected situations, and cultivate mental strength. This resilience instills an unwavering confidence in your own capabilities, which is fundamental to feeling empowered in all areas of life.

Confidence: Confidence is the key to empowerment. In the practice of Krav Maga, it is forged through a series of small victories and gradual improvement. As you become skilled in various techniques, confront your fears, and build a strong mind-body bond, you will gain a deep sense of self-assurance. This newfound confidence will extend beyond the training space, enabling you to confront any obstacle with bravery and unwavering resolve.

Focus: Empowerment is all about staying focused and being present in the moment. In Krav Maga, you'll discover how to direct your attention and energy towards swiftly and efficiently dealing with threats. This increased focus goes beyond training, boosting your ability to be productive and perform well in all areas of life.

Stress Relief: Krav Maga is an incredible way to find stress relief. Through physical training, you are able to release all the built-up tensions and emotions. This helps you manage stress effectively, leading to emotional balance, improved mental well-being, and a feeling of empowerment.

Discipline and Self-Control: Discipline is key to feeling empowered, as it allows for regular practice and a commitment to getting better. Krav Maga helps you develop discipline and self-control, which leads to making wise choices and managing your impulses, both in and out of training.

Mindfulness: Enhancing self-awareness and emotional regulation is key to empowerment. By practicing Krav Maga, you can develop mindfulness, which allows you to be present, observe your thoughts and feelings, and respond thoughtfully instead of impulsively reacting. This mindfulness can positively influence your daily life, leading to more empowered and mindful decision-making.

Communication and Relationship: Effective communication and positive relationships are key to empowerment in the Krav Maga community. When we communicate clearly and respectfully, we build trust and camaraderie, creating a training environment that is supportive and empowering.

Introspection: Self-reflection and introspection play a crucial role in personal development and empowerment within the realm of Krav Maga. When you take the time to examine your motivations, recognize your strengths, and acknowledge areas for improvement, you are able to customize your training journey to successfully achieve your goals and elevate yourself to new levels of empowerment.

> *"Empowerment isn't just having strength, it's harnessing it with purpose, vision, and heart."*

Mind-Body Connection: Empowerment is all about connecting your mind and body, and you can achieve this through Krav Maga training. By breathing in sync with your movements, imagining yourself succeeding, and building mental strength, you can create a balanced connection between your physical and mental selves, unlocking your true potential.

Embracing Fear: By confronting your fears and learning how to handle high-pressure situations, you can develop emotional strength and a strong belief in your ability to overcome any challenge.

Visualization: Empowerment is reinforced through visualization, as you mentally rehearse success and envision achieving your goals. By visualizing yourself as empowered individuals, both in Krav Maga and in everyday life, you manifest your potential and become architects of your destiny.

Emotional Regulation: Empowerment entails managing emotions effectively, and Krav Maga provides a platform for emotional regulation in challenging situations. By remaining composed and making informed decisions under pressure, you demonstrate empowerment through emotional intelligence.

Gratitude: Gratitude is the key to empowerment in Krav Maga. By appreciating your progress, your training partners, and the supportive Krav Maga community, you will feel motivated, positive, and connected to the empowering practice.

Leadership: Empowerment and leadership are closely linked. As you embark on your journey of empowerment, it is important to inspire and support others along the way. By setting a good example, treating others with respect, and creating a positive and inclusive training environment, you uplift not only yourself but the entire community.

Krav Maga Nurtures Empowerment

Krav Maga brings about positive changes in your life. Through its special techniques, philosophies, principles, teaching methods, and focus on real-life situations, Krav Maga helps you become more empowered. This section will explore how Krav Maga contributes to your personal development and confidence, both during training and in your everyday life.

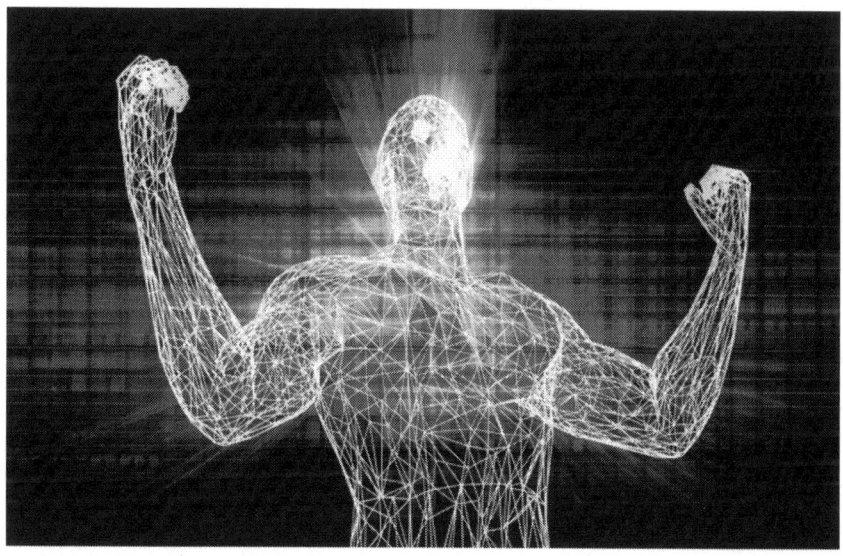

Techniques: Krav Krav Maga techniques are specifically created to protect you in real-life situations, making you feel empowered and ready for any potential danger. For instance, you'll learn how to defend yourself against common street attacks like punches, kicks, and grabs. Through regular practice, these techniques become second nature, giving you the confidence to respond quickly and efficiently when confronted with such threats.

Krav Maga also emphasizes de-escalation strategies and assertive communication. By mastering these techniques, you'll be able to defuse confrontations verbally and establish clear boundaries, empowering yourself to avoid physical conflicts whenever possible.

Concepts & Philosophies: In the world of Krav Maga, your self-confidence, determination, and personal growth come first. One important principle is to "neutralize the threat," which means believing in your ability to take charge in dangerous situations and keep yourself and others safe. This mindset helps you become a strong and fearless individual who can tackle any challenge.

Krav Maga also encourages using everyday objects as improvised weapons. This concept teaches you to think outside the box and adapt to different situations, giving you the power to defend yourself creatively.

Principles: The Two key principles of Krav Maga - empowerment and effectiveness. Krav Maga aims to equip individuals with simple, efficient techniques that can be easily recalled and employed in high-pressure situations. For instance, in Krav Maga's "combatives" training, emphasis is placed on a small number of powerful strikes and kicks that enable one to swiftly incapacitate an attacker and make a swift exit to safety. Another crucial principle in Krav Maga is "360-degree awareness," which underscores the significance of being alert to one's surroundings at all times. By maintaining situational awareness, individuals empower themselves to identify potential threats early and proactively take measures to ensure their own safety.

Teaching Methods: Krav Maga focuses on empowering individuals, regardless of their experience or background.

Instructors cultivate an inclusive and motivating atmosphere that values your growth and development. They offer personalized guidance and feedback to enhance your skills and boost your self-confidence. During partner exercises, instructors promote positive reinforcement and constructive criticism to foster a strong sense of camaraderie and empowerment. This approach ensures that every individual's progress is recognized and supported.

Reality-Based Focus: Krav Maga's Krav Maga's focus on real-world situations not only prepares you physically for confrontations but also strengthens your mental responses. One way it does this is through stress drills, which simulate high-pressure situations to help you develop emotional control and mental toughness. This enables you to think clearly and act decisively even in stressful situations.

> *"Krav Maga teaches that true empowerment is born from preparedness, resilience, and the undying spirit to rise above."*

Another aspect of Krav Maga is its scenario-based training. Practitioners role-play different real-life situations, allowing you to practice your techniques and problem-solving skills in practical ways. This helps build your confidence and preparedness in your everyday life.

Krav Maga empowers you by boosting your self-confidence, resilience, and assertiveness. Through this practice, you develop a growth mindset, continually improving yourself and believing in your abilities. The skills and mindset you gain on the training mat transfer to your everyday life, allowing you to tackle challenges with confidence and inner strength. Krav Maga empowers you not only for self-defense but also to become a leader and positive role model in your community. By embracing these empowering principles, you unleash your full potential and take control of your own success.

Ripples of Empowerment

Krav Maga has a lasting positive impact on many areas of your life. As you become more confident, resilient, and open-minded, these qualities affect your relationships, career, mental health, and overall well-being. They also have a wider impact on society.

> *"Empowerment from Krav Maga resonates beyond its techniques; it's the confidence to navigate life's battles with poise and purpose."*

Let's take a look at some real-life examples to see how empowerment can truly transform these different aspects.

Personal Relationships: Empowerment through Krav Maga can have a positive impact on your relationships with loved ones, friends, and colleagues. When faced with conflicts or disagreements, you will be better equipped to approach discussions assertively and empathetically, which can promote healthy communication and understanding. Being empowered in this way allows you to be a source of support for others, helping them conquer their own fears and challenges by sharing your own experiences in overcoming obstacles through Krav Maga. This can create stronger bonds and contribute to the development of a strong support network.

Professional Life: Krav Maga not only empowers you physically, but it also has a positive impact on your professional life. By practicing Krav Maga, you will become more confident and disciplined, which will influence your decision-making and goal-setting in your career. You will feel more comfortable taking calculated risks and seizing opportunities for advancement. For instance, with the confidence and discipline gained from Krav Maga, you may feel capable of applying for a leadership position. You will know that you have the skills to overcome challenges and be an influential role model. Additionally, this newfound confidence will enable you to negotiate assertively for a higher salary and seek out more opportunities for career growth.

Mental Health Benefits: Krav Maga helps boost self-esteem, build resilience, and develop effective coping strategies. Through training, you learn to conquer fears and grow personally, which in turn increases self-confidence and reduces negative self-talk.

Mastering self-defense techniques and confronting fears in Krav Maga training gives you a sense of achievement and self-belief. As you overcome challenges on the mat, you gain confidence in handling difficult situations in other areas of life.

Additionally, Krav Maga provides a way to release stress and emotions. The intense training allows you to channel your emotions in a positive way, relieving pent-up stress and anxiety. The discipline and focus required during training also help cultivate mindfulness, promoting emotional regulation and overall well-being.

Empowerment through Krav Maga equips you with the skills to navigate life's ups and downs. It enhances your adaptability and resilience, enabling you to seek out support and resources when needed, recognizing the importance of mental well-being and self-care.

Physical Health Implications: Krav Maga training instills discipline in various areas of physical health, such as fitness routines and dietary choices. By empowering yourself, you develop a consistent exercise routine, understanding how important physical fitness is for self-defense and overall well-being. This includes setting specific fitness goals and working towards achieving them, which gives you a sense of accomplishment and motivation to maintain a healthy lifestyle. Additionally, Krav Maga focuses on functional strength, agility, and cardiovascular endurance, which encourages you to participate in complementary exercises and cross-training to improve your overall physical abilities.

But Krav Maga doesn't stop at physical fitness. It also promotes healthy eating habits that support your training and overall health. Through empowerment, you become aware of the importance of proper nutrition in fueling your body for intense workouts and aiding in recovery. As you develop a strong mind-body connection through Krav Maga, you become more in tune with your body's needs and consciously make choices to prioritize your health and well-being. Moreover, the stress-relieving aspect of Krav Maga contributes to improved physical health. Regular training sessions offer an outlet for releasing tension and pent-up emotions, which promotes relaxation and reduces the risk of stress-related health problems.

Physical fitness, good nutrition, and stress relief have a great impact on your well-being. They boost your energy levels, improve your sleep, and strengthen your immune system. The practice of Krav Maga empowers you and forms the basis for a healthier and more dynamic lifestyle. It helps you take control of your physical health and become a role model in your community. These aspects not only affect your physical well-being but also have a significant impact on your mental health.

The Larger Societal Impact: Empowerment through Krav Maga can lead to a broader societal impact as you become an agent of positive change within your community and beyond. As a leader and mentor, you have the opportunity to teach vulnerable populations how to protect themselves and promote safety measures in your neighborhood. Your actions and sense of responsibility can inspire others to take action as well.

Krav Maga's empowering principles have a domino effect, transforming not only yourself but also the world around you. By improving your mental and physical well-being and cultivating inner strength, you can live a more fulfilling life and motivate others to embark on their own journey of self-discovery and growth. Together, we can create a stronger, safer, and more resilient community, united by courage, resilience, and a commitment to personal development.

Conclusion

Krav Krav Maga is a life-changing journey that empowers you in every aspect of your life. It teaches discipline, resilience, emotional control, and leadership skills, which help you overcome challenges and grow personally. Krav Maga not only boosts your confidence but also changes your mindset to see opportunities instead of limitations. As you train and improve, this empowerment becomes a powerful force that drives you towards a fulfilling and meaningful life. It also improves your relationships, teaching you to work together, trust others, and build a supportive community. By embracing empowerment, you become a catalyst for change both in your own life and in the world.

CHAPTER 20

Mensch On A Mat

"In the realm of Krav Maga, being a mensch means being a force for positive change, treating others with respect, maintaining humility and unwavering integrity in our pursuit of growth."

GM Dr. Neil Farber

Welcome to the chapter on "Mensch on a Mat." In this section, we explore the essence of integrity, compassion, and altruism within the context of Krav Maga and its impact on personal growth, resilience, and fostering a strong sense of community. Embracing the qualities of a mensch not only enhances our abilities as Krav Maga practitioners but also enriches our lives beyond the training mat.

The Meaning of Mensch

A mensch is someone with outstanding character traits that make them worthy of admiration and respect. The word comes from Yiddish and is often used to describe someone who is truly kind, trustworthy, and dependable. Being a mensch means more than just doing nice things occasionally - it means consistently having a good and selfless nature.

Let's take a look at what are considered qualities of being a mensch.

- **Kindness** is at the heart of a mensch. They consistently show compassion and empathy towards others, offering genuine support and care, even in challenging situations. Their goal is to uplift and encourage those around them.
- **Honesty** is another fundamental aspect of being a mensch. They value integrity and uphold principles of truthfulness. This earns them the trust and admiration of others, as they are seen as reliable and dependable.

- **Integrity** is a quality that sets mensches apart. They consistently exhibit moral courage and principled behavior, staying true to their values and principles even when faced with difficult decisions. This unwavering commitment to doing what is right is truly inspiring.
- Lastly, **altruism** is a defining trait of a mensch. They give selflessly to others, making a positive impact on their community and beyond. Their contribution to the well-being of others is guided by a genuine desire to make the world a better place.

> *"To be a mensch is to recognize that our legacy isn't measured by accolades, but by the lives we touch, uplift, and inspire."*

Being a mensch, or a person of integrity and kindness, not only affects your own well-being but also has a positive impact on building a strong community. By embodying mensch qualities, you will find a deeper sense of fulfillment and purpose in your life. Acts of kindness and selflessness not only improve your emotional state and reduce stress but also create a sense of connection with others. As a mensch, you play a vital role in creating a supportive and compassionate community. Your presence and actions inspire others to embrace similar qualities, resulting in a harmonious environment. This sense of unity extends beyond the boundaries of a specific group or activity, enriching all aspects of life for everyone involved.

Mensch on the Mat

In the world of Krav Maga, ethical behavior and integrity are essential. They shape the training experience, creating an environment of growth, camaraderie, and respect. Krav Maga instructors emphasize ethical conduct, encouraging students to embody these qualities both inside and outside the training arena.

Being a Krav Maga practitioner requires discipline and respect. As you progress, you learn to respect your instructors, training partners, and the art itself. This respect extends to valuing the safety and well-being of others, fostering a trusting and supportive environment.

> *"With every stance and strike in Krav Maga, there's a whisper of menschhood; reminding us that our greatest strength lies in our character, our compassion, and our commitment to elevate those around us."*

Discipline improves technique and cultivates mental attributes like self-control and perseverance.

Krav Maga training presents challenging scenarios that test physical and mental limits. It teaches compassion, fairness, and responsibility. These values become the foundation of your moral compass, guiding ethical decisions both in training and everyday life. Personal responsibility extends beyond the mat, encouraging a mensch-like approach to all aspects of life. Krav Maga helps develop this moral compass through challenges and upholding values.

By incorporating ethics and integrity into your Krav Maga training, you not only become a skilled martial artist but also a person of good character - someone who inspires and uplifts others both within the Krav Maga community and in the wider world.

Krav Maga teaches you the importance of giving back to society and helping others. Many Krav Maga schools and organizations organize community service projects and charitable events, giving you the opportunity to make a positive contribution. Whether you're teaching self-defense to vulnerable groups or fundraising for local causes, these acts of kindness and service cultivate a supportive and compassionate Krav Maga community.

Engaging in altruistic acts within the Krav Maga community brings a deep sense of purpose and fulfillment. By helping others improve their self-defense skills and confidence, you become a force for positive change in their lives and find your own sense of purpose. This sense of purpose extends beyond the training room, enriching your own life as you experience the joy of making a difference and positively impacting those around you.

Research has proven that being kind to others and lending a helping hand can greatly impact your mental well-being and ability to handle tough situations. By giving back, your body releases chemicals like oxytocin that make you feel good, reducing stress and promoting happiness. Moreover, being selfless creates a feeling of connectedness and belonging within the Krav Maga community, which strengthens your mental resilience and makes it easier to face challenges.

When you take the opportunity to help others, you not only embody the qualities of a good person but also experience personal growth and satisfaction. This means that your journey with Krav Maga becomes about making a positive impact on the lives of others and creating a community that supports and cares for each other.

Living as a Mensch

Becoming a good person goes beyond just training in Krav Maga. It means incorporating qualities like kindness, honesty, integrity, and altruism into all areas of your life, including work, family, and social interactions. By consistently embodying these qualities, you can have a positive influence on those around you and contribute to a supportive community. Developing these qualities through Krav Maga training can also improve your relationships with others. Treating people with respect and compassion builds trust and deepens connections. Being honest and having integrity enhances your credibility and reliability.

As a good person, you can inspire and positively impact those you meet. Everyone wants to be around someone who is kind and considerate because it just feels good. People may even hope that some of those good qualities will rub off on them. Being a good person also empowers you to face life's challenges with integrity and compassion. When difficult situations arise, you approach them with fairness and empathy. By staying true to your moral compass and making ethical choices, you not only maintain your self-respect but also inspire others to do the same. Embracing personal growth and development becomes natural when you're committed to being a good person, as you constantly strive to improve and make a positive impact in the world.

> *"In Krav Maga, every lesson extends beyond self-defense to self-discovery, nurturing mensches who champion values, respect, and genuine human connection."*

As you embody the qualities of a mensch in your daily life, you become a shining example of positive character and a catalyst for positive change in your community. By embracing kindness, honesty, and selflessness, you contribute to creating a better and more caring world, where everyone reaps the rewards of your mensch-like behavior. The mental benefits of practicing Krav Maga go beyond just self-defense, empowering you to make a positive impact and advocate for the well-being of others.

Mensch Mindset

By adopting a mensch mindset, you can experience a profound transformation in your mental resilience and personal growth. The essence of being a mensch lies in practicing kindness, honesty, integrity, and altruism, which in turn shapes a positive and empowering outlook on life. With this mindset, you are better equipped to navigate the challenges that come your way with grace and compassion, as well as develop inner strength and fortitude to overcome obstacles and thrive in the face of adversity.

One of the key benefits of embracing the mensch mindset is enhanced coping abilities. When confronted with difficult situations, your commitment to ethics and compassion becomes a source of support, allowing you to find meaning and purpose even in the toughest of times. Rather than surrendering to negativity or despair, the mensch mindset encourages you to seek solutions and learn from challenges. By cultivating emotional intelligence and empathy, you form strong connections with others, creating a support system that aids in your coping process.

> *"Krav Maga doesn't just craft fighters; it molds mensches; champions of integrity, empathy, and unwavering purpose on and off the mat."*

Furthermore, the mensch mindset is inherently growth-oriented, fueled by a desire for continuous improvement and making a positive impact on the world. As a mensch, you welcome challenges as opportunities for learning and growth. Your dedication to personal development and ethical behavior gives you the strength to confront setbacks with resilience, utilizing them as stepping stones towards self-improvement. By nurturing your mensch mindset, you cultivate the mental flexibility to adapt to change and the determination to confront obstacles head-on, ultimately fostering personal growth that extends beyond the boundaries of physical training, such as Krav Maga.

Being a mensch, or a person of integrity and compassion, can greatly enhance your mental resilience and personal growth. By practicing ethical behavior, developing effective coping mechanisms, and adopting a growth-oriented mindset, you will be better equipped to navigate life's difficulties and make a positive contribution to both yourself and others. The mensch mindset is a powerful tool that empowers you to confront adversity with courage, strength, and a dedication to making a meaningful difference in the world.

Conclusion

In the world of Krav Maga, being a mensch means embodying humility, integrity, respect, and kindness both during training and in daily life. Through the rigorous training and values taught in Krav Maga, we are encouraged to become mensches - individuals who have strong moral character and show empathy and leadership.

Krav Maga offers a transformative journey to becoming a mensch by promoting self-awareness, emotional control, and the connection between mind and body. We learn to face our fears, build inner strength, and develop a sense of gratitude, which helps us handle challenges with resilience and composure.

Being a mensch goes beyond just training - it positively impacts our personal relationships, professional endeavors, and overall well-being. Off the training floor, the mensch mindset encourages open communication, empathy, and a sense of community, leading to more fulfilling interactions with loved ones, friends, and colleagues.

Both in Krav Maga and in life, being a mensch creates a ripple effect of positive change. It not only promotes personal growth but also inspires others to embody the same virtues, creating a collective force for a better world. Embracing the qualities of a mensch empowers us to lead by example, make ethical choices, and contribute to a compassionate and resilient society. As Krav Maga practitioners and mensches, we are not only capable protectors but also advocates for a more connected world.

CHAPTER 21

Krav Warrior Mindset

"With the Krav Warrior Mindset, obstacles become stepping stones, fear becomes fuel, and determination becomes an unstoppable force."

Dr. GM Neil Farber

In this (almost) final chapter, we will explore the core of a Krav warrior's mindset. Throughout this book, we have discussed various key elements, and now we will bring them together. The Krav Warrior Mindset goes beyond just improving your fighting and self-defense skills. Yes, that is important, but it also has a broader impact on your overall happiness and success in life. We will delve into goal-oriented thinking, maintaining a positive attitude, being adaptable, managing fear, and building emotional resilience. By integrating these pillars, you will develop a powerful Krav warrior mindset. Understanding how all these components work together will reveal the true essence of mental strength and empowerment in Krav Maga. So, let us embark on this transformative journey to master the art of being a Krav warrior, both inside and outside the training arena.

Goal-Oriented

Developing a Krav Warrior Mindset requires being goal-oriented. In Krav Maga, setting clear and specific objectives is crucial for staying focused and driven in your training. Whether your goals involve mastering techniques, improving stamina, or advancing through belt levels, having well-defined targets helps keep you motivated and committed to your progress. Without proper goal setting, your aspirations will remain as mere dreams that are unlikely to come true. Psychology expert Dr. Neil Farber emphasizes the importance of setting realistic and optimistic goals, complete with concrete timelines and deadlines. Taking action and consistently working towards these goals is what transforms dreams into achievable milestones.

Krav Maga training teaches you the significance of setting up small goals along the way, much like dominoes falling in a chain. Each successful accomplishment pushes you forward, building momentum towards your ultimate objectives. By breaking down bigger aspirations into manageable steps, you create a sense of progress and accomplishment. This, in turn, strengthens your determination to keep pushing forward.

In his book, Dr. Farber emphasizes the importance of setting goals that have a strong underlying value, a clear purpose and a "WHY". For example, wanting to improve in

Krav Maga is more meaningful when it is coupled with a reason like wanting to protect loved ones. This intrinsic motivation forms the basis of commitment, giving your goals greater significance.

> *"In the pursuit of greatness, the Krav Warrior Mindset knows no limits, transforming potential into purpose."*

Visualization, which is discussed in Chapter 14, is a powerful tool for being goal-oriented. By mentally rehearsing your training sessions and picturing successful outcomes, you boost your confidence and reinforce your dedication to achieving your objectives. Visualizing yourself overcoming challenges strengthens your belief in your abilities and prepares your mind for success.

Training in Krav Maga cultivates the discipline and perseverance needed to pursue your goals. The demanding and challenging nature of the practice builds determination, and as you consistently put in effort, you develop the resilience to go beyond your limits. As you witness your progress and experience triumphs in Krav Maga, this goal-oriented mindset naturally extends to other areas of your life.

Krav Maga teaches you how to set goals and achieve them, not only in training but in all areas of life. By learning to establish clear objectives and develop actionable plans, you can turn your dreams into reality. This mindset makes you more proactive in seeking opportunities for growth and success. By setting specific goals and creating strategies to achieve them, you increase your chances of fulfillment and achievement in all aspects of life.

Having a Krav Warrior Mindset means approaching life with purpose and determination. Through Krav Maga training, you learn how to set goals, overcome obstacles, visualize success, and make continuous progress. By breaking your journey into smaller dominoes that you can knock over with a swift front kick, staying focused on your values and motivations, you pave the way for personal growth, resilience, and accomplishment. The power of purposeful goal setting fuels the Krav Warrior Mindset, driving you to thrive as a capable, focused, and determined individual. It becomes a transformative force that propels you towards excellence.

Optimistic

A Krav Warrior Mindset is all about being optimistic. It means having a positive outlook that helps you face challenges with hope and confidence. In Krav Maga, optimism goes beyond just being positive - it's a mental attitude that believes you can overcome obstacles and thrive in tough situations. When you train in Krav Maga, you develop this optimistic mindset and it brings many benefits beyond just the training itself.

Research has shown that optimistic people have better immune systems, stronger relationships, perform better at work, and even live longer. When you approach Krav Maga training with optimism, you're more likely to push yourself beyond what you think you can do, strive for constant improvement, and stay positive even when things don't go your way.

> *"In the arena of life, the Krav Warrior Mindset fearlessly faces challenges, transforming adversity into opportunity."*

Optimism in Krav Maga isn't about ignoring the challenges of self-defense training. It's about believing in your own growth and development. As you progress in your training, you become more resilient, and this optimism spills over into other areas of your life. The confidence you gain from overcoming physical and mental challenges in Krav Maga carries over to your personal and professional life too.

Optimistic people make fewer mistakes because they see setbacks and failures as opportunities to learn. In Krav Maga, every mistake is a chance to grow and become better. By staying positive during tough training sessions, you develop a strong mental resilience to tackle challenges with composure. This positive mindset also helps you build better relationships with your training partners and instructors. It creates a supportive community of like-minded individuals who are all passionate about self-improvement.

This positive attitude carries over into your everyday life, enhancing your interactions with others. Embracing optimism through Krav Maga not only benefits your fighting spirit but also improves your overall well-being. It boosts your immune system, strengthens your relationships, increases your success at work, and even has the potential to lengthen your life. The Krav Warrior Mindset is a powerful tool that empowers you to face life's challenges with unwavering positivity, resilience, and a belief in your potential for greatness.

Adaptable and Flexible

At the heart of the Krav Warrior Mindset is the importance of being adaptable and flexible. In Krav Maga, these qualities extend beyond just physical techniques. They encompass the ability to adjust and respond effectively to the constant changes and demands of life. By embracing adaptability and flexibility in your training, you cultivate a resilient mindset that empowers you to succeed in any situation.

In Krav Maga, adaptability means understanding that every encounter is unique. You learn to tailor your responses and techniques based on the specific circumstances and variables involved. This adaptive approach ensures that you can effectively defend yourself, no matter how unpredictable the situation may be.

Flexibility in Krav Maga encompasses both the physical and mental aspects. Physically, you develop agility, speed, and the ability to move effortlessly in response to threats. Mentally, you are open to new ideas, willing to learn from others, and capable of considering different solutions. This mental flexibility allows you to explore various approaches and adjust your strategies for the best possible outcomes.

> *"The Krav Warrior Mindset embraces the unknown, for in uncertainty lies the realm of infinite possibilities."*

Krav Maga training can improve your ability to think on your feet and adapt to new situations. By simulating real-life scenarios and adding stress, you can learn to overcome challenges and become more mentally flexible. This mental agility doesn't just benefit you in self-defense; it also helps you navigate unexpected changes in everyday life, like adjusting to a new job or dealing with personal setbacks. Being adaptable and flexible in these situations allows you to seize opportunities and continue growing. In the professional world, this flexibility can help you respond to challenges, adapt to market demands, and propel your career forward with confidence.

In personal relationships, these qualities make communication and problem-solving better, which leads to stronger connections with others. Being open to different perspectives helps create harmony and trust.

Being adaptable and flexible also helps with mental well-being. Embracing change and uncertainty reduces anxiety and stress. Having a flexible mindset makes you stronger and more determined in the face of tough times.

Overall, being adaptable and flexible in both Krav Maga and life gives you confidence to tackle any situation. By adopting the Krav Warrior Mindset, you learn to adapt and thrive in life's challenges and opportunities.

Manages Fear

The Krav Warrior Mindset goes beyond conquering fear, it involves learning to manage and embrace it. In Krav Maga, fear is acknowledged as a natural response to danger but it doesn't paralyze you. Instead, fear becomes a catalyst for action, helping you respond effectively in high-stress situations. Krav Maga training teaches you to use fear as strength, allowing you to thrive in combat and in life.

Fear management in Krav Maga means acknowledging fear without letting it control you. Through rigorous training, you become familiar with the sensations and emotions fear brings. You learn to control your breathing, stay focused, and make rational decisions even under pressure. By exposing yourself to stressful scenarios in a safe environment, you develop the mental resilience needed to confront fear head-on.

Embracing fear in Krav Maga doesn't mean seeking danger. It means acknowledging its presence and using it to heighten your alertness and responsiveness. Fear sharpens your instincts, helping you detect threats and react quickly. This heightened awareness becomes a valuable skill, making you more vigilant in your surroundings and better equipped to protect yourself and others.

> *"A true Krav Warrior knows that victory is not just surviving the fight, but also conquering the fears within."*

The art of Krav Maga teaches you a powerful mindset shift that helps you conquer fear in all aspects of life. Instead of freezing or panicking when faced with fear, you learn to take decisive action. This mental shift has countless benefits, especially in professional settings.

For those in leadership roles, public speaking can often be anxiety-inducing. However, with the Krav Warrior Mindset, you learn to embrace the rush of adrenaline and use it to deliver captivating presentations. Managing fear allows you to connect with your audience and make a lasting impact.

In competitive environments, fear management gives you an edge. For example, if you work in sales and negotiating deals is a crucial part of your job, fear of rejection or failure can hinder your performance. But with Krav Maga training, you stay composed and think strategically even under pressure. This allows you to enter negotiations with confidence, build stronger relationships with clients, and increase your success rate in closing deals.

Overall, Krav Maga training not only helps you protect yourself physically, but also empowers you to handle any challenge that comes your way with poise and composure.

In everyday life, managing fear can greatly improve relationships and build emotional strength. Let's focus on how this applies to our relationships with loved ones. During difficult conversations or conflicts, fear of confrontation may have caused you to avoid discussing important issues. However, by adopting the Krav Warrior Mindset, you approach these situations differently. You recognize your fear and use it as motivation to address problems in a constructive manner. This newfound ability to manage fear opens up channels of communication, leading to more meaningful and honest exchanges with your partner, family, and friends.

Furthermore, fear management also affects your personal growth. It allows you to embrace challenges that once seemed overwhelming. For instance, starting a new hobby or pursuing further education may have appeared daunting before, but now you view them as opportunities for growth and learning. The Krav Maga mindset has provided you with the mental strength to tackle these challenges, stepping out of your comfort zone and reaping the rewards of personal development.

The Krav Warrior Mindset makes you feel powerful and resilient by helping you conquer your fears. It teaches you to accept fear as a normal part of life and use it as motivation to take action. As a result, you become better at communicating, making decisions, and showing compassion. The mental strength you gain from Krav Maga training goes beyond just physical fitness, making you stronger and more confident in all areas of your life..

Resilient

Resilience is a crucial characteristic of a Krav Warrior Mindset. It goes beyond physical endurance to include mental strength and the ability to bounce back from challenges. In Krav Maga, resilience is not about how often you fall down, but about how many times you get back up and keep fighting. This unwavering determination to persevere in the face of adversity is what defines a true warrior. While every high-level Krav Maga instructor teaches resilience, when I think of Krav Maga training that is focused on enhancing resilience, Dr. Itay Gil comes to mind. With his extensive training of Israeli Counter Terror Fighters he has created a methodology to not just pressure-test but to "crash test" to the point of failure. This subject is so important in Krav Maga and in all areas of life that Dr. Gil and I are currently working on a resilience book.

In Chapter 3, we discussed the benefits of resilience. Now, let's explore resilience in the context of a Krav Warrior Mindset. Krav Maga training exposes you to difficult and stressful situations, both physically and mentally. You learn to surpass your limits and embrace discomfort as a means of personal growth. The path to mastering self-defense techniques is filled with struggles and setbacks, but each obstacle presents an opportunity to learn and improve.

By cultivating resilience, you develop the necessary skills to face challenges head-on and continue fighting despite adversity.

Resilience is deeply ingrained in the Krav Warrior Mindset. During training, you face challenges head-on, facing opponents who may be stronger or more skilled. Instead of being disheartened by losses or mistakes, you view them as valuable learning experiences. This resilience enables you to adapt and refine your techniques, making you a more effective and formidable fighter.

> *"Empowered by the Krav Warrior Mindset, we forge our destiny on the anvil of resilience and self-belief."*

Beyond the training mat, this resilience serves as a powerful asset in various aspects of life. In a professional setting, you approach setbacks with a solution-oriented mindset. Let's say you face a project that encounters unexpected roadblocks. Rather than giving in to frustration or defeat, your resilient nature drives you to reevaluate the situation and seek alternative approaches to achieve your goals.

Resilience also plays a crucial role in career progression. Promotions or opportunities for advancement may not come easily, but your ability to persevere and continue striving positions you as a top candidate for growth within your organization. Employers value individuals who can handle pressure and adapt to change, making your resilient attitude a sought-after asset in the workplace.

Resilience is crucial in our personal lives. It helps us build stronger relationships and enhances our emotional well-being. When faced with challenging times like a troubled relationship or a personal loss, our ability to bounce back and stay strong is essential. By offering unwavering support and staying resilient, we build deeper connections with those around us, earning their trust. Imagine a situation where your relationship is going through a rough patch. Instead of giving up, your resilient mindset pushes you to communicate openly and work through the issues together. You approach conflicts with empathy, seeking resolution rather than playing the blame game. This resilience doesn't just help you survive tough times; it also strengthens the foundation of your relationship, creating a profound bond based on trust and mutual support.

Resilience is the secret to navigating life's unpredictable moments. It allows you to remain calm and focused when faced with unexpected challenges, such as financial or health issues. By developing resilience, you can approach these situations with a clear mind and find effective solutions. For instance, let's say you suddenly find yourself in a financial crisis due to unforeseen expenses. Being resilient empowers you to stay composed and devise a plan to overcome the setback, rather than succumbing to fear and panic. With resilience, you gain the strength to seek guidance, explore new possibilities, and create a roadmap for recovery. It instills a sense of confidence, knowing that you possess the inner strength to overcome any obstacle life throws your way.

Additionally, resilience helps you develop a positive view of life. Even when faced with hardships, you maintain hope and optimism, understanding that challenges are temporary and can lead to personal growth. This positive mindset not only benefits you but also influences those around you. Your resilience becomes an inspiration to your loved ones, friends, and colleagues, motivating them to face their own challenges with bravery and determination.

In times of crisis, your resilient nature shines through as a guiding light for others. For example, during the COVID-19 pandemic, your ability to adapt to changing circumstances, maintain emotional stability, and find ways to stay connected with loved ones became a source of strength for your community. Your resilient attitude fosters a sense of unity and hope, reminding others that they too can overcome difficulties and emerge stronger.

The Krav Warrior Mindset of resilience empowers you to tackle life's challenges with grace and strength. Embrace challenges as opportunities for growth, keep a positive outlook, and support those around you. Your resilience becomes an inspiration and brings transformation to your personal sphere. Through Krav Maga training and a resilient mindset, you become a symbol of unwavering strength, empowering yourself and others to face life's uncertainties with determination and courage.

Emotionally In Control

Emotional control is a crucial part of the Krav Warrior Mindset. It helps you utilize your emotions instead of letting them control you. In your Krav Maga training, you learn to understand and work with your emotional responses. This allows you to use them in a positive and productive way. It's important to note that emotional control doesn't mean suppressing your emotions. Instead, it means acknowledging and effectively managing them.

Emotional control is especially important when it comes to training and real-life self-defense situations. When faced with a confrontational opponent or a high-pressure situation, staying emotionally grounded allows you to think clearly and make smart decisions. For example, if you're sparring with a tough opponent, being calm and focused helps you analyze their movements, find weaknesses, and respond with accuracy.

> *"Mentally fortified, the Krav Warrior Mindset remains composed under pressure, turning chaos into calculated action."*

Emotional control has many benefits outside of just the training mat. It helps you handle conflicts and challenges professionally at work, and prevents impulsive reactions to criticism. In personal relationships, it fosters healthier communication and understanding during disagreements. Additionally, emotional control helps with decision-making, ensuring that fear or anxiety doesn't drive rash choices. Instead, you can objectively evaluate options and choose what aligns with your long-term goals and values.

Emotional control also plays a role in managing stress and promoting overall well-being. By developing the capacity to regulate emotions effectively, you reduce the negative impact of stress on your mind and body. This, in turn, enhances your physical and mental health, allowing you to perform better in all aspects of life.

The Krav Warrior Mindset helps you take charge of your emotions instead of being controlled by them. By learning to understand and handle your emotions in a positive way, you improve your ability to tackle problems, make wise choices, and create stronger connections with others. Krav Maga training is like a training ground for developing emotional control. It equips you with the necessary skills to apply this valuable ability to all aspects of your life. This leads to personal growth and helps you become the best version of yourself.

Accountability

In Chapter 2, I discussed the concept of accountability, and how it was enhanced by training in Krav Maga. In this section, I'll focus on how accountability is a crucial element of the Warrior Mindset. It involves taking responsibility for your actions, decisions, and outcomes. Accountability is the first habit in Dr. Stephen Covey's renowned "7 Habits of Highly Effective People" and the first "Key" in Dr. Neil Farber's transformative "8 Keys to Achieve." By embracing accountability in both Krav Maga and life, you empower yourself to take control of your progress and personal growth.

In the world of Krav Maga, accountability is instilled right from the beginning. As you embark on your training journey, you learn to set clear goals and targets and hold yourself accountable for achieving them. It is important to recognize your strengths and weaknesses, continuously striving to improve and evolve as a practitioner. Krav Maga instructors encourage self-reflection and provide feedback, creating a culture of accountability within the training environment.

Through Krav Maga, you develop a sense of ownership over your progress. You understand that growth requires dedication and commitment. Being accountable in training means consistently showing up, challenging yourself to excel, and adhering to high standards of discipline. When you take ownership of your development, you become the master of your success, and each accomplishment becomes a testament to your unwavering dedication.

Being accountable means fulfilling your duties, meeting deadlines, and taking responsibility for your contributions in professional settings. It earns you the trust and respect of colleagues, paving the way for professional growth.

In your personal life, accountability strengthens relationships and builds trust. When you hold yourself accountable for your words and actions, you become a person of integrity. You follow through on commitments and take responsibility for mistakes. This level of accountability creates a solid foundation for meaningful connections with others.

> *"With the Krav Warrior Mindset, accountability becomes a powerful beacon, illuminating the path to personal growth and self-mastery."*

Accountability also plays a crucial role in pursuing personal goals and hobbies. Whether it's improving a skill, indulging in creative pursuits, or maintaining a healthy lifestyle, being accountable pushes you to stay committed.

For instance, if you set a goal to practice mindfulness every day, being accountable means sticking to the commitment, even in the face of distractions or obstacles.

Accountability forms a vital part of the Warrior Mindset, embodying responsibility and ownership. Krav Maga fuels the development of this essential quality, fostering self-discipline and self-improvement. By embracing accountability in training and everyday life, you become an empowered and respected individual, guiding your own destiny with purpose and determination. The journey of the Warrior Mindset transcends Krav Maga, influencing all areas of life and empowering you to be proactive and accomplished in the pursuit of excellence.

Putting It All Together: Thriving with the Krav Warrior Mindset

The Krav Warrior Mindset is all about thriving in every aspect of our lives. Through Krav Maga training, we develop a powerful mindset that allows us to face life's challenges with strength, resilience, and adaptability. With this mindset, we can achieve our goals, visualize success, and turn our dreams into reality. Optimism is a key element, attracting success and fostering meaningful relationships. Being adaptable and flexible helps us find solutions even in difficult times. Resilience allows us to bounce back stronger from setbacks, and regulating our emotions enables us to respond effectively in high-stress situations. Finally, accountability makes us reliable and trustworthy, empowering us to make a positive impact on others and ourselves.

> *"With the tenacity of a Krav Maga warrior, every obstacle becomes an invitation to rise, to conquer, to thrive."*

With each component interwoven into the Krav Warrior Mindset, you become a powerful force, transcending the boundaries of the training mat. This powerful mindset enriches all areas of your life, making you more than just a Krav Maga practitioner – it transforms you into a thriving individual who lives life fully.

In the professional realm, you become a standout leader who inspires and guides others toward greatness. In personal relationships, your empathy, emotional intelligence, and communication skills nurture profound connections, making you a cherished presence in the lives of loved ones. As you pursue hobbies and personal goals, the Krav Warrior Mindset fuels your passion, unleashing your potential for greatness

The Krav Warrior Mindset is like a compass that helps you navigate through life, leading you to success, fulfillment, and happiness. It transforms you into someone who not only survives life's challenges but also flourishes in the face of difficulty. Keep in mind that this mindset is not a final destination, but rather an ongoing journey of personal growth and self-discovery. It is a precious gift that you carry with you, empowering you to overcome any obstacle with undying strength, resilience, and bravery. With this mindset, you have the power to design a life that is thriving and fulfilling in every aspect.

CHAPTER 22

Conclusion

"May the teachings of 'Krav Mind' be your beacon, lighting the path of self-awareness, fortitude, and boundless aspiration, on and off the mat."

Dr. GM Neil Farber

Recap of Mental Benefits

In this book, we have explored the many ways in which practicing Krav Maga can greatly improve our mental well-being, resilience, and personal growth. Now, let's quickly recap some of the key mental benefits we've discussed in the previous earlier chapters.

1. **Accountability** - The power of personal responsibility and goal-setting, as Krav Maga training fosters a sense of ownership and commitment to continuous self-improvement.
2. **Resilience** - The ability to bounce back from adversity and thrive in challenging situations, as Krav Maga empowers you to overcome obstacles and cultivate mental toughness.
3. **Confidence** - Unshakable self-assurance as you master self-defense techniques, building a strong

belief in your capabilities both on and off the training mat.

4. **Focus** - Sharpen your mental clarity and situational awareness, enhancing your ability to make quick decisions and stay composed under pressure during Krav Maga training and everyday life.
5. **Stress Relief** - Therapeutic benefits of physical activity and mindfulness, as Krav Maga provides an outlet for stress release and equips you with tools to manage anxiety.
6. **Discipline and Self-Control** - The mental fortitude to stay committed to your goals, manage distractions, and maintain self-control, enhancing overall discipline in various areas of life.
7. **Mindfulness** - Staying present, focused, and composed during training, applying these techniques to manage emotions and achieve clarity in daily life.
8. **Communication** - Verbal and non-verbal communication skills, fostering effective interactions and mutual respect with training partners and in personal relationships.
9. **Relationships** - Strong connections within the Krav Maga community, cultivating camaraderie and trust, and applying these skills to nurture meaningful relationships outside of training.
10. **Introspection** - self-reflection and personal growth, as Krav Maga training becomes a journey of self-discovery and understanding.
11. **Mind-Body Connection** - The link between your physical and mental capabilities, recognizing how

mental strength enhances physical performance and vice versa.
12. **Embracing Fear** - Embracing and managing fear, transforming it into a driving force for personal growth and empowerment in all aspects of life.
13. **Visualization** - Harnessing the power of mental rehearsal and positive visualization to enhance performance and build confidence in Krav Maga and beyond.
14. **Empathy** - Cultivating empathy and emotional intelligence, developing a deeper understanding of others and enhancing your ability to connect and communicate effectively.
15. **Emotional Regulation** - Mastering emotional control and resilience, enabling you to respond to challenges with composure and make rational decisions even in high-stress situations.
16. **Gratitude** - Fostering gratitude as a powerful tool for mental well-being, stress reduction, and emotional regulation, cultivating a deeper sense of interconnectedness and personal growth in all aspects of your life.
17. **Leadership** - Transformative principles of Krav Maga that shape not just proficient fighters but compassionate, resilient, and visionary leaders in life.
18. **Empowerment** - Embracing a sense of empowerment and independence as you learn to protect yourself and others through Krav Maga training, fostering confidence and self-worth.
19. **Mensch** - Krav Maga's teachings that go beyond technique, highlighting the importance of integrity,

compassion, and true mensch values in all aspects of life.
20. **Krav Warrior Mindset** - Unite the mental benefits of Krav Maga, forging a warrior mindset that empowers you not only in self-defense but also in personal growth, happiness, and fulfillment.

By understanding and accepting the mental benefits of Krav Maga, you can tap into its life-changing potential. This martial art is more than a brilliant self-defense system; it offers a holistic approach to personal growth and mental strength. The journey of self-improvement doesn't stop with this book; it is an ongoing process that goes beyond these pages. As you apply the principles of Krav Maga in your everyday life, you become more than just a practitioner—you become a Krav Warrior, ready to succeed in all areas of your life.

Integration and Transformation:

Krav Maga training can transform you both mentally and physically. In this book, I've explored the mental benefits that come with practicing Krav Maga. As you immerse yourself in the training, you'll find these benefits seamlessly integrating into every aspect of your life.

One of the first mental changes you will experience is a sense of accountability. Taking ownership of your training and progress will help you develop a proactive mindset. This mindset will extend beyond the training mat and into other areas of your life. You will start setting clear goals and breaking them down into achievable steps, and you will have a clear understanding of why these goals are important to you. This sense of responsibility will also extend to your professional aspirations and relationships, allowing you to achieve your dreams.

Resilience is another important aspect of Krav Maga training. Through this training, you will learn to bounce back from setbacks and embrace challenges. Instead of seeing failure as defeat, you will see it as an opportunity for growth and learning. This resilience will empower you to face obstacles head-on and turn adversity into stepping stones toward success.

Krav Maga boosts your confidence, helping you tackle life's uncertainties with self-assurance. This translates into professional success, as you become adept at handling high-pressure situations. In personal relationships, you communicate confidently, respecting boundaries and expressing your needs effectively.

The practice of focus and mindfulness keeps you present and attentive, improving your decision-making skills in all aspects of life. This heightened awareness allows you to navigate daily challenges with clarity and control.

Krav Maga training also instills discipline and self-control. You become better at managing your time and staying committed to your goals, even in the face of distractions. This newfound discipline leads to healthier habits, including better eating, regular exercise, and overall improved well-being.

Additionally, Krav Maga empowers you emotionally, fostering a greater sense of empathy and emotional intelligence. You become more attuned to others' emotions, leading to stronger connections and more meaningful relationships. Understanding and embracing your own emotions also enables you to be a better communicator and a compassionate listener.

Krav Maga training is about transforming your mindset into that of a Krav Warrior. This mindset empowers you to face challenges in all areas of your life with courage, resilience, and adaptability. By embracing the principles and practices of Krav Maga you can unleash your hidden potential and achieve greater success and fulfillment. This book serves as a reminder to integrate these principles into your daily life and allow Krav Maga to guide you towards becoming the best version of yourself. By harnessing the mental and physical synergy of Krav Maga, you will develop the mental fortitude needed to conquer any challenge and thrive in all aspects of your life.

Empowerment and Personal Growth

Krav Maga empowers practitioners mentally. Through training, you experience personal growth and develop the belief in your abilities. This newfound confidence extends to other areas of your life, allowing you to embrace challenges and pursue your goals with determination.

Krav Maga provides a platform for continuous personal growth by pushing you beyond your comfort zone. As you conquer challenges and witness your progress, you gain self-assurance and motivation to take on new obstacles. This empowerment fosters independence and self-reliance, freeing you from self-doubt and fear.

The mental benefits of Krav Maga have a positive impact outside of training. In professional settings, the sense of empowerment translates into assertiveness and resilience, making you a more confident and proactive team member or leader. You become adaptable, finding innovative solutions to challenges and approaching tasks with a growth-oriented mindset. In personal relationships, the empowerment gained from Krav Maga enhances your ability to communicate effectively, setting healthy boundaries, and cultivating deeper connections with others. You become an advocate for your own needs, making choices that align with your values and goals. As a result, your relationships become more fulfilling and authentic, fostering a sense of belonging and support.

Krav Maga has tremendous impact on your mental well-being. By practicing Krav Maga, you develop emotional intelligence, gaining a better understanding and control over your emotions. This leads to healthier expression of emotions and improved interpersonal relationships. You also experience personal growth, as Krav Maga helps you identify your values and set meaningful goals. This sense of purpose allows you to pursue activities that bring joy and contentment to your life. Moreover, Krav Maga empowers you to embrace change, overcome challenges, and take personal responsibility for your actions. This mental fortitude enables you to tackle obstacles, reach your goals, and lead a resilient and purposeful life. By embracing the principles of Krav Maga and harnessing its mental and physical synergy, you can transform your life for the better. So, embrace the empowerment, growth, and resilience that Krav Maga provides and become the best version of yourself.

Real-Life Application

Let's review some real-life scenarios where the mental benefits of Krav Maga can be applied:

- *Personal Conflict Resolution*: Conflicts are inevitable. Inevitably, conflicts arise in our lives. By applying the communication and emotional intelligence techniques developed in Krav Maga, you can effectively handle disagreements while showing empathy and assertiveness. Through this process, you will master the art of active listening, recognizing different perspectives, and discovering constructive solutions. As a result, your relationships will become more harmonious, and you will achieve more productive outcomes.
- *Stress Management*: In the midst of our busy lives, stress can be a constant battle we face. However, practicing Krav Maga can help us effectively manage this stress. By developing focus and mindfulness through training, we gain valuable tools for staying calm, recognizing what triggers our stress, and utilizing relaxation techniques to regain a sense of balance.
- *Decision Making*: The mental discipline and problem-solving skills acquired through Krav Maga carry over effortlessly into our everyday lives. When faced with significant decisions, the experiences gained from this training help us evaluate risks, consider advantages and disadvantages, and ultimately make informed choices with unwavering certainty.
- *Confidence Building*: The confidence and empowerment gained from Krav Maga practice extends to all aspects of your life. Whether it is public speaking, pursuing a new career path, or taking on leadership roles, the self-assurance developed in

training allows you to step out of your comfort zone and embrace opportunities for growth.
- *Personal Safety*: The situational awareness and safety mindset instilled in Krav Maga training increases your personal safety in everyday life. From recognizing potential threats in public spaces to establishing safety protocols at home, you'll take proactive measures to protect yourself and the people you care about.
- *Resilience in Adversity*: Life has its highs and lows, but practicing Krav Maga helps you develop mental toughness to recover from setbacks. You'll see challenges as chances to learn and improve, maintain your determination through adversity, and come out even stronger, ready to achieve your goals.
- *Time Management*: Incorporate the goal-setting and discipline practiced in Krav Maga into your daily time management. You'll prioritize tasks, set achievable deadlines, and staying focused on important responsibilities, maximizing productivity and achieving a healthier work-life balance.
- *Empathy and Understanding*: Empathy developed in partner drills and training experiences, allows you to better understand and appreciate other people's perspectives. Interactions with others will become more compassionate, fostering a stronger sense of connection and harmony in your relationships.
- *Conflict Avoidance*: Use the de-escalation techniques taught to defuse dangerous situations in your daily life to peacefully navigate difficult encounters, minimizing conflicts and promoting positive interactions.

- *Goal Achievement*: In Krav Maga, we develop a mindset focused on achieving goals. Whether you want to explore a new hobby, further your education, or enhance your health and fitness, the discipline and determination cultivated in Krav Maga will help you succeed in reaching your dreams.
- *Conflict Resolution at Work*: In the fast-paced world of work, conflicts arise between colleagues or bosses. By drawing on communication and emotional intelligence skills from Krav Maga, you can actively listen to others' viewpoints, stay calm during heated discussions, and team up to find win-win solutions creating a great work environment.
- *Dealing with Road Rage*: While driving, you may encounter aggressive or rude drivers triggering road rage. Apply Krav de-escalation techniques to calmly diffuse tense situations on the road. Instead of reacting with anger, you'll maintain self-control, avoid confrontation, and prioritize the safety of yourself and others.
- *Public Speaking*: Even the most confident people can find public speaking intimidating. By drawing on self-assurance, empowerment, and deep breathing techniques gained from Krav Maga, you'll face these challenges as opportunities with confidence; effectively getting your message across.
- *Parenting Challenges*: Parenting can be tough and stressful. Use stress management techniques from Krav Maga, to handle the pressures of being a parent. You'll stay calm, think clearly, and react with patience

and understanding when faced with difficult situations involving your children.
- *Negotiation Skills*: Whether negotiating a salary, a business deal, a major purchase, or deciding who's going to take out the garbage, the decision-making and problem-solving skills acquired in Krav Maga enhance your negotiation abilities. You'll have a strategic edge, address the needs and concerns of both parties, and work towards mutually beneficial outcomes.

Incorporating the mental advantages of Krav Maga into real-life situations improves your own well-being and creates a positive ripple effect in your interactions and relationships with others. Krav Maga's transformative power enables you to live a life full of mental strength, resilience, and personal development.

The Journey Continues

As you apply the mental skills gained from Krav Maga to real-life situations, remember that the journey never ends. Keep challenging yourself, strive for self-improvement, and integrate the principles of accountability, resilience, and empowerment into your daily life and into everything you do. By harnessing the mental benefits of Krav Maga you can lead a life defined by mental strength, confidence, and the ability to thrive in any situation.

This book is just the beginning of your journey towards self-improvement and mental well-being. Just as Krav Maga advances with each training session, you too can grow and develop in your personal development. When faced with life's challenges, approach them with the same determination and bravery you bring to your Krav Maga practice.

Use the lessons from Krav Maga to develop a mindset of continuous learning and adaptability. Be open to new opportunities, seek out fresh challenges, and step out of your comfort zone to broaden your mental horizons. Remember, progress isn't always straightforward; there will be ups and downs, and each experience presents a chance to learn and improve.

Surround yourself with a supportive community of like-minded people who are passionate about mental well-being and personal growth. Engage in discussions, share experiences, and learn from each other. The Krav Maga community goes beyond the training center, offering wisdom and encouragement from fellow practitioners. Joining FIMA - The Federation of Israeli Martial Arts (www.theFIMA.com) is a great way to be part of this supportive community of like-minded individuals passionate about Krav Maga.

It's also important to take time for self-reflection. Assess your mental strengths and areas for improvement, and set realistic and meaningful goals for your personal journey. Celebrate your successes and use setbacks as opportunities to build resilience. Remember that the mental principles you learn in Krav Maga are interconnected and shape your mindset in all areas of life. Embrace your inner warrior not just during training, but in every aspect of your life.

Personal growth is a lifelong commitment, so embrace the journey. Each step forward brings new insights and challenges that help you understand yourself better. With the mental benefits of Krav Maga, you can face life's uncertainties with courage, self-assurance, and a positive outlook - the Krav Warrior mindset. You will also embrace empathy, integrity, honesty and compassion - a true mensch.

Let Krav Maga transform your life by strengthening your mental resilience, fostering personal growth, and bringing lasting fulfillment. Embrace the ever-evolving warrior within you and face any challenges that come your way.

Gratitude and Farewell

As we come to the end of this book, I want to express my sincere thanks to all of you, the readers, and the Krav Maga community as a whole. Your dedication to exploring the mental aspects of Krav Maga and your commitment to personal growth truly inspire me. I am grateful that you have joined me in this journey to discover the many mental benefits of Krav Maga. I hope that the insights and strategies shared in these pages have resonated with you and have given you the confidence and resilience that Krav Maga fosters.

I also want to thank the Krav Maga community for creating such a supportive and empowering environment. Your passion for personal growth, mental well-being, and self-defense has made this community strong and welcoming to people from all walks of life. Together, we stand united and share a commitment to developing mental strength and becoming the best versions of ourselves.

As you continue your Krav Maga journey, I encourage you to hold onto the principles and values we have explored in this book. Embrace the challenges that come your way, take responsibility for your growth, and keep moving forward with strength and confidence. Always carry with you the mindset of a Krav warrior – believe in your abilities and have the courage to face any obstacles that come your way. In moments of doubt, draw upon the mental skills you've honed through Krav Maga to stay strong and resolute. The world is full of opportunities for growth and self-improvement. Embrace every experience as a chance to deepen your understanding of yourself and the world around you. I am confident that your path will lead to remarkable successes and transformative experiences.

Thank you for being a part of this book and for embracing the mental dimensions of Krav Maga with open hearts and minds. May your life be forever enriched by the Krav Warrior Mindset that you carry within you.

Keep training, keep growing, and enjoy the journey of self-improvement through Krav Maga.

References

When it comes to Krav Maga and its connection to mental health, there is a lack of literature. Consequently, most of the references mentioned in the following chapters are about related subjects. Chapter 1 is an exception and provides a list of highly recommended books that cover various aspects of Krav Maga, such as principles, philosophies, techniques, and strategies.

Note: All *"quotations"* in the book that are not referenced, are taken from the writings of Dr. GM Neil Farber (with permission).

Chapter 1: Krav Mind

1. Sde-Or Imi, Yanilov E. (2001). *Krav Maga: How to Defend Yourself Against Armed Assault*. Frog Books. This is one of, if not *the* first comprehensive books on Krav Maga by Imi Lichtenfeld, who brought Krav Maga to the civilian population and one of his top disciples, Eyal Yanilov.
2. Kahn D. (2004). *Krav Maga: An Essential Guide to the Renowned Method – For Fitness and Self-Defense*. St. Martin's Griffin. This is one of the first books written in English about Krav Maga and it covers many of the

important facets including targets, weapon defense, and self-defense escapes.
3. Kahn D. (2008). *Advanced Krav Maga: The Next Level of Fitness and Self-Defense*. St. Martin's Griffin. This book by the Chief US Instructor for the Israeli Krav Maga Association, explores essential combative tactics including the mindset of effective self-defense.
4. Kahn D. (2015). *Krav Maga Defense: How to Defend Yourself Against the 12 Most Common Unarmed Street Attacks*. St. Martin's Press. This book teaches how to gain the upper hand in the 12 most common unarmed street attacks the average person is likely to encounter.
5. Evans, G. (2016). *Krav Maga: The Best Guide to Over 50 Self-Defense Moves for Women and Men*. Independently Published. Very basic ebook about the principle and techniques. Free download available for those new to Krav Maga.
6. Ben Keren, G. (2017). *Krav Maga Tactical Survival: Personal Safety in Action.* Tuttle Publishing. EPUB. Great book for practical tactical information. Available as free download.
7. Kahn D. (2019). *Krav Maga Combatives: Maximum Effect*. YMAA Publication Center. This book is designed for krav maga trainees, civilians, law enforcement officers, security professionals, and military personnel who want to improve their chances of surviving a hostile attack.
8. Whitman J. (2020). *Krav Maga. Black Belt*. Wren Publications. While this book focuses on advanced, black belt techniques, it does a great job reviewing basic foundational principles as they relate to higher level strategies.

9. Yanilov E, Boe O. (2020). *Krav Maga – Combat Mindset & Fighting Stress*. Meyer & Meyer Sport; Illustrated edition. An excellent book written by a senior Krav Maga Grandmaster focusing on cutting-edge techniques and training methods that can be employed under high-stress conditions.
10. Kahn D. (2021). *Krav Maga Fundamental Strategies*. YMAA Publication Center. This book by a true master in Krav Maga is full of practical, battle-tested strategies, tactics, and insights.
11. Levine D, & Whitman J. (2022). *Complete Krav Maga: The Ultimate Guide to Over 250 Self-Defense and Combative Techniques*. Ulysses Press. This book is based on the foundational Krav Maga principles and includes techniques and strategies from beginner yellow belt to advanced black belt.
12. Levine D, Whitman J, Hoover R. (2022). *Krav Maga for Beginners: A Step-By-Step Guide to the World's Easiest-to-Learn, Most-Effective Fitness and Fighting Program*. This book presents the fundamental techniques and most useful real-world moves.
13. Nystrom T. (2023). *May the Skill Be With You: How to Accelerate Skill Acquisition in SELF-DEFENSE*. Book Cover – Finland. Excellent book, focusing on applying principles to accelerate Krav Maga learning.

Chapter 2: Accountability

1. Covey SR. (1989). *The 7 Habits of Highly Effective People: Powerful Lessons in Personal Change*. Simon & Schuster. This book by Stephen Covey is a classic in personal development literature and discusses the importance of

taking responsibility for one's actions and choices as a key element of personal effectiveness.
2. Robbins T. (1992). *Awaken the Giant Within: How to Take Immediate Control of Your Mental, Emotional, Physical, and Financial Destiny.* Simon & Schuster. In this book, Tony Robbins discusses the role of accountability in taking control of one's life and achieving personal transformation.
3. Farber N. (2014). *The Blame Game: The Complete Guide to Blaming. How to Play and How to Quit.* Dynamic Publishing Group. This book provides you with the knowledge, tools, and inspiration you need to accept responsibility and gain control of your life.
4. Katz DA. (2017). *The Power of Accountability: Turning 'What If' into 'What Is'.* ForbesBooks. This book explores the concept of accountability in personal and professional contexts, discussing how being accountable can lead to greater success and fulfillment in life.
5. Farber N. (2018). *Throw Away Your Vision Board: The Truth About the Law of Attraction.* Lioncrest Publishing. In this book, Neil Farber challenges the conventional wisdom of vision boards and encourages readers to focus on taking action and being accountable for their goals rather than simply visualizing them.
6. Brown B. (2018). *Dare to Lead: Brave Work. Tough Conversations. Whole Hearts.* Random House. Brené Brown's book emphasizes the importance of vulnerability, honesty, and accountability in leadership and personal growth.

Chapter 3: Resilience

1. Luthar SS, Cicchetti D, & Becker B. (2000). *The Construct of Resilience: A Critical Evaluation and Guidelines for Future Work.* Child Development, 71(3), 543-562. In this comprehensive review, Suniya Luthar, Dante Cicchetti, and Bronwyn Becker critically evaluate the construct of resilience and provide guidelines for future research in the field.
2. Masten AS, & Reed MG. (2002). *Resilience in Development.* Handbook of Positive Psychology, 74-88. In this chapter from the "Handbook of Positive Psychology," Ann Masten and Margaret Reed explore the concept of resilience in human development and the factors that promote resilience across the lifespan.
3. Bonanno GA. (2004). *Loss, Trauma, and Human Resilience: Have We Underestimated the Human Capacity to Thrive After Extremely Aversive Events?* American Psychologist, 59(1), 20-28. This research article by George Bonanno discusses the human capacity for resilience after experiencing traumatic events and the factors that contribute to resilience.
4. Levine D, Whitman J. (2007). *Complete Krav Maga: The Ultimate Guide to Over 230 Self-Defense and Combative Techniques.* Ulysses Press. This book introduces the concept that Krav Maga principles can be applied to business and other aspects of life. In addition to overcoming obstacles, this book also discusses awareness training, operating under stress, and transferring knowledge from instructor to student.
5. Meichenbaum D. (2007). *Resilience and the Brain: Using Cognitive Techniques to Build Resilience.* Psychotherapy,

44(3), 360-373. This article by Donald Meichenbaum discusses the role of cognitive techniques in building resilience and coping with stress and adversity.
6. Southwick SM, & Charney DS. (2018). *Resilience: The Science of Mastering Life's Greatest Challenges.* Cambridge University Press. This book delves into the scientific aspects of resilience, exploring how individuals can develop and cultivate resilience to cope with various challenges in life.
7. Gil I, Farber NE. (2020). *The Ultimate Stress Test. Lessons learned from the Yamam Israeli Counter-Terror Team.* www.PsychologyToday.com, The Blame Game Blog. 2-24-20.
8. Gil I, Farber NE. (2020). *Failing Your Way to Success: Stress to Resilience.* www.PsychologyToday.com, The Blame Game Blog. 3-9-20.

Chapter 4: Confidence

1. Bandura A. (1994). *Self-efficacy.* In V. S. Ramachandran (Ed.), Encyclopedia of human behavior (Vol. 4, pp. 71-81). Academic Press. This seminal work by Albert Bandura introduces the concept of self-efficacy, which plays a crucial role in building confidence and belief in one's abilities.
2. Woodman T, & Hardy L. (2001). *A Case Study of Organizational Stress in Elite Sport.* Journal of Applied Sport Psychology, 13(3), 207-228. While this study focuses on stress in elite sport, it also discusses the role of confidence in managing pressure and maintaining performance under challenging conditions.
3. Hattie J. (2012). *Visible Learning for Teachers: Maximizing Impact on Learning.* Routledge. In this book, John Hattie

discusses various factors that influence student achievement, including the impact of self-confidence and self-belief on learning outcomes.
4. Hall A. (2019). *Confidence: How to Overcome Your Limiting Beliefs and Achieve Your Goals*. Random House Business. In this book, Adrian Hall offers practical strategies and insights for building confidence and overcoming limiting beliefs that hinder personal growth.
5. Cuncic A. (2021). *The Link Between Confidence and Mental Health*. Verywell Mind. This article explores the relationship between confidence and mental health, highlighting the importance of building self-assurance for overall well-being.

Chapter 5: Focus

1. Lutz A, Slagter HA, Dunne JD, & Davidson RJ. (2008). *Attention regulation and monitoring in meditation*. Trends in Cognitive Sciences, 12(4), 163-169. This research article examines the relationship between meditation, attention regulation, and cognitive control, highlighting how mindfulness practices can enhance focus and concentration.
2. Goleman D. (2013). *Focus: The Hidden Driver of Excellence*. HarperCollins. This book explores the science of attention and concentration, discussing how focus impacts various aspects of our lives, including performance, relationships, and personal well-being.
3. Mrazek MD, Franklin MS, Phillips DT, Baird B, & Schooler JW. (2013). *Mindfulness training improves working memory capacity and GRE performance while reducing mind wandering*. Psychological Science, 24(5), 776-781. This research paper discusses how mindfulness training can

enhance working memory and cognitive performance, which can be related to the benefits of focus and concentration in Krav Maga.
4. Lebeau RB, & Mesagno C. (2016). *Cognitive and attentional processes in competitive contexts*. In Progress in Brain Research (Vol. 227, pp. 221-244). Elsevier. This chapter provides insights into the cognitive and attentional processes involved in competitive contexts, including sports and self-defense situations, which can be relevant to the topic of focus in Krav Maga.
5. Loh SY, Lee SH, & Murray NP. (2018). *The effects of anxiety and attentional control on visual search in skilled field hockey players*. Psychology of Sport and Exercise, 37, 174-181. This study explores how anxiety and attentional control influence visual search skills in skilled athletes, offering insights into the importance of focus in high-stress situations.

Chapter 6: Stress Relief

1. Velicer WF, Diclemente CC, Rossi JS, & Prochaska JO. (1990). *Relapse situations and self-efficacy: An integrative model*. Addictive Behaviors, 15(3), 271-283. doi: 10.1016/0306-4603(90)90070-E - This study presents an integrative model exploring how self-efficacy and relapse situations interact, shedding light on how stress relief techniques like Krav Maga may enhance individuals' belief in their ability to cope with challenging situations.
2. Breus MJ, & O'Connor PJ. (1998). *Exercise-induced anxiolysis: A test of the "time out" hypothesis in high anxious females*. Medicine & Science in Sports & Exercise, 30(7), 1107-1112. doi: 10.1097/00005768-199807000-00011 -

Examining the effects of exercise on anxiety levels, this research provides insights into how engaging in Krav Maga as a form of physical activity can lead to anxiolysis and stress reduction.

3. Stanton AL, Kirk SB, Cameron CL, & Danoff-Burg S. (2000). *Coping through emotional approach: Scale construction and validation.* Journal of Personality and Social Psychology, 78(6), 1150-1169. doi: 10.1037/0022-3514.78.6.1150 - This study contributes to the understanding of coping mechanisms, including emotional approaches, which aligns with how Krav Maga training helps individuals manage stress and respond effectively to challenging situations.

4. Hofmann SG, Asnaani A, Vonk IJ, Sawyer AT, & Fang A. (2012). *The Efficacy of Cognitive Behavioral Therapy: A Review of Meta-analyses.* Cognitive Therapy and Research, 36(5), 427-440. doi: 10.1007/s10608-012-9476-1 - While not specific to Krav Maga, this review of meta-analyses underscores the efficacy of cognitive-behavioral approaches in managing stress and anxiety, supporting how the mental discipline cultivated in Krav Maga can be beneficial in stress relief and overall mental well-being.

5. Zschucke E, Renneberg B, Dimeo F, Wüstenberg T, & Ströhle A. (2015). *The stress-buffering effect of acute exercise: Evidence for HPA axis negative feedback.* Psychoneuroendocrinology, 51, 414-425. doi: 10.1016/j.psyneuen.2014.10.019 - Exploring the stress-buffering effects of acute exercise on the HPA axis, this research supports the notion that Krav Maga, as a physically demanding practice, can be effective in

reducing stress by regulating the body's stress response system.

Chapter 7: Discipline and Self-Control

1. Levine D, & Hoover R. (2009). *Krav Maga for Beginners: A Step-by-Step Guide to the World's Easiest-to-Learn, Most-Effective Fitness and Fighting Program*. This book delves into the principles and techniques of Krav Maga, including how discipline and self-control play vital roles in mastering the martial art.
2. Duhigg C. (2012). *The Power of Habit: Why We Do What We Do in Life and Business*. While not specifically about Krav Maga, this book explores the science of habits and how discipline and self-control are essential in forming positive habits and breaking bad ones.
3. McGonigal K. (2012). *The Willpower Instinct: How Self-Control Works, Why It Matters, and What You Can Do to Get More of It*. This book delves into the science of willpower and self-control, providing insights and strategies to strengthen these mental attributes.
4. Ben Keren G. (2016). *Krav Maga: Real World Solutions to Real World Violence*. This book covers various aspects of Krav Maga, including the mental aspects of discipline and self-control that are crucial in mastering the art.
5. Gil I, Farber NE. (2020). *The Ultimate Stress Test. Lessons learned from the Yamam Israeli Counter-Terror Team*. www.PsychologyToday.com, The Blame Game Blog. 2-24-20.
6. Yanilov E, Boe O. (2020). Krav Maga – Combat Mindset & Fighting Stress. Meyer & Meyer Sport; Illustrated edition. An excellent book written by a senior Krav Maga Grandmaster focusing on cutting-edge training

methods that can be employed under high-stress conditions.
7. Whitman J. (2020). *Krav Maga. Black Belt*. Wren Publications. While this book focuses on advanced, black belt techniques, it does a great job reviewing basic foundational principles as they relate to higher level strategies.
8. Kahn D. (2021). *Krav Maga Fundamental Strategies*. YMAA Publication Center. This book by a true master in Krav Maga is full of practical, battle-tested strategies, tactics, and insights.
9. Levine D, & Whitman J. (2022). *Complete Krav Maga: The Ultimate Guide to Over 250 Self-Defense and Combative Techniques*. Ulysses Press. This book is based on the foundational Krav Maga principles and includes techniques and strategies from beginner yellow belt to advanced black belt.
10. Levine D, Whitman J, Hoover R. (2022). *Krav Maga for Beginners: A Step-By-Step Guide to the World's Easiest-to-Learn, Most-Effective Fitness and Fighting Program*. This book presents the fundamental techniques and most useful real-world moves.
11. Nystrom T. (2023). *May the Skill Be With You: How to Accelerate Skill Acquisition in SELF-DEFENSE*. Book Cover – Finland.

Chapter 8: Mindfulness

1. Langer EJ. (1990). *Mindfulness*. Addison-Wesley. In this seminal book, Ellen Langer explores the concept of mindfulness and its potential to transform our perception and experience of the world, offering practical insights into living more mindfully.

2. Kabat-Zinn J. (1994). *Wherever You Go, There You Are: Mindfulness Meditation in Everyday Life.* Hyperion. This classic book by Jon Kabat-Zinn introduces readers to the concept of mindfulness and provides practical techniques for integrating mindfulness into daily life.
3. Brown KW, & Ryan RM. (2003). *The benefits of being present: Mindfulness and its role in psychological well-being.* Journal of Personality and Social Psychology, 84(4), 822-848. doi: 10.1037/0022-3514.84.4.822. This research paper examines the link between mindfulness and psychological well-being, highlighting its positive impact on overall mental health.
4. Davidson RJ, Kabat-Zinn J, Schumacher J, Rosenkranz M, Muller D, Santorelli SF, ... Sheridan JF. (2003). *Alterations in brain and immune function produced by mindfulness meditation.* Psychosomatic Medicine, 65(4), 564-570. doi: 10.1097/01.PSY.0000077505.67574.E3. This study investigates the effects of mindfulness meditation on brain activity and immune function, revealing potential physiological benefits.
5. Raposa ML. (2003). *Meditation and the Martial Arts.* Univ. of Virginia Press. This book discusses the use of meditation both to prepare for combat and as a form of combat in various martial arts (it does not include Krav Maga).
6. Davis DM, & Hayes JA. (2011). *What are the benefits of mindfulness? A practice review of psychotherapy-related research.* Psychotherapy, 48(2), 198-208. doi: 10.1037/a0022062. This comprehensive review explores the benefits of mindfulness practices, including

improved emotional regulation, reduced stress, and increased well-being.

7. Hölzel BK, Lazar SW, Gard T, Schuman-Olivier Z, Vago DR, & Ott U. (2011). *How does mindfulness meditation work? Proposing mechanisms of action from a conceptual and neural perspective.* Perspectives on Psychological Science, 6(6), 537-559. doi: 10.1177/1745691611419671. This research article delves into the mechanisms behind mindfulness meditation, providing insights into its effectiveness in promoting well-being and emotional regulation.

8. Kabat-Zinn J. (2013). *Full Catastrophe Living: Using the Wisdom of Your Body and Mind to Face Stress, Pain, and Illness.* (Bantam). From one of the first mindfulness experts in the west. Great book for applying mindfulness to promote well-being.

9. Bluestein D. (2018). *Mindfulness in Action: Making Friends with Yourself through Meditation and Everyday Awareness.* Shambhala Publications.

10. Yanilov E, Boe O. (2020). *Krav Maga – Combat Mindset & Fighting Stress.* Meyer & Meyer Sport; Illustrated edition. An excellent book written by a senior Krav Maga Grandmaster focusing on cutting-edge training methods that can be employed under high-stress conditions.

11. Kahn D. (2021). *Krav Maga Fundamental Strategies.* YMAA Publication Center. This book by a true master in Krav Maga is full of practical, battle-tested strategies, tactics, and insights.

12. Levine D, & Whitman J. (2022). *Complete Krav Maga: The Ultimate Guide to Over 250 Self-Defense and Combative*

Techniques. Ulysses Press. This book is based on the foundational Krav Maga principles and includes techniques and strategies from beginner yellow belt to advanced black belt.

13. Langer EL (2023). *The Mindful Body: Thinking Our Way to Chronic Health*. Da Capo Lifelong Books. Excellent book by Harvard mindfulness professor. Ellen Langer is one of the pioneers of mindfulness research. Her work is far from esoteric and can be easily applied to everyday life.

Chapter 9: Communication

1. Johnson DW, & Johnson RT. (1995). *Learning Together and Alone: Cooperative, Competitive, and Individualistic Learning* (5th ed.). Allyn & Bacon. This book explores the dynamics of cooperative and competitive learning, providing insights into effective communication within group settings.
2. Goleman D. (1996). *Emotional Intelligence: Why It Can Matter More Than IQ*. Bantam Books. Goleman's groundbreaking work on emotional intelligence highlights the significance of emotional awareness and communication skills in building successful relationships.
3. Hargie O. (2011). *Skilled Interpersonal Interaction: Research, Theory, and Practice* (5th ed.). Routledge. This comprehensive resource delves into the theory and practice of skilled interpersonal interaction, offering valuable insights into effective communication techniques.
4. Patterson K, Grenny J, McMillan R, & Switzler A. (2012). *Crucial Conversations: Tools for Talking When Stakes Are High* (2nd ed.). McGraw-Hill Education. This book offers practical strategies for effective communication during

crucial conversations, providing tools for handling difficult discussions and resolving conflicts constructively.
5. DeVito JA. (2017). *The Interpersonal Communication Book* (14th ed.). Pearson. DeVito's book provides a comprehensive overview of interpersonal communication, covering topics such as verbal and non-verbal communication, active listening, and conflict resolution.

Chapter 10: Relationships

1. Reis HT, & Shaver P. (1988). *Intimacy as an interpersonal process.* In S. W. Duck (Ed.), Handbook of personal relationships: Theory, research and interventions (pp. 367-389). John Wiley & Sons. This academic chapter delves into the concept of intimacy as a crucial aspect of interpersonal relationships, highlighting its role in fostering trust and emotional closeness.
2. Uchino BN. (2009). *Understanding the links between social support and physical health: A lifespan perspective with emphasis on the separability of perceived and received support.* Perspectives on Psychological Science, 4(3), 236-255. doi: 10.1111/j.1745-6924.2009.01122.x. This review article explores the relationship between social support and physical health, emphasizing the importance of both perceived and received support in promoting well-being throughout the lifespan.
3. Simon-Thomas ER, Godzik J, Castle E, Antonenko O, Ponzio A, Kogan A, & Keltner DJ. (2016). *An fMRI study of caring vs self-focus during induced compassion and pride.* Social Cognitive and Affective Neuroscience, 11(4),

541-549. doi: 10.1093/scan/nsv132. This study examines brain activity during compassionate and prideful experiences, revealing the neurobiological basis of positive emotions in social relationships.
4. Beebe J, Beebe S, & Ivy D. (2019). *Communication: Principles for a Lifetime*. Pearson. This comprehensive textbook explores the principles of effective communication, including the importance of trust and cooperation in building strong relationships.
5. Johnson SM. (2019). *Attachment theory in practice: Emotionally Focused Therapy (EFT) with individuals, couples, and families*. The Guilford Press. This book delves into emotionally focused therapy and attachment theory, providing insights into how secure emotional bonds and relationships contribute to overall mental health and well-being.

Chapter 11: Introspection

1. Ryan, RM, & Deci EL. (2001). *On Happiness and Human Potentials: A Review of Research on Hedonic and Eudaimonic Well-Being*. Annual Review of Psychology, 52(1), 141-166. doi: 10.1146/annurev.psych.52.1.141. This review explores the concepts of hedonic and eudaimonic well-being, shedding light on the importance of self-reflection and personal growth for overall happiness and fulfillment.
2. Park CL. (2010). *Making Sense of the Meaning Literature: An Integrative Review of Meaning Making and Its Effects on Adjustment to Stressful Life Events*. Psychological Bulletin, 136(2), 257-301. doi: 10.1037/a0018301. This integrative review examines the role of meaning-making in coping with stressful life events, underscoring the

significance of introspection and finding purpose in challenging circumstances.
3. Morin A. (2011). *Self-Reflection and Academic Performance: Is There a Relationship?* Social Psychology of Education, 14(3), 367-379. doi: 10.1007/s11218-011-9157-y. This study investigates the connection between self-reflection and academic performance, highlighting the role of introspection in enhancing learning and self-awareness among students.
4. Sugiura Y, Sugiura T, & Croft DB. (2015). *Meditation and Self-Reflection: A Phenomenological Study of Buddhist Practitioners' Experiences.* Journal of Psychology and Theology, 43(3), 177-189. This phenomenological study delves into the experiences of Buddhist practitioners engaging in meditation and self-reflection, providing insights into the transformative nature of introspective practices.
5. Zeng X, Chiu CPK, Wang R, Oei TPS, & Leung FYK. (2019). *The Effectiveness of a Mindfulness-Based Intervention in Promoting Emotional Regulation, Self-Reflection, and Self-Awareness among Chinese Adolescents with Substance Use Disorder: A Randomized Controlled Trial.* Mindfulness, 10(4), 759-771. doi: 10.1007/s12671-018-1047-0. This study explores the impact of a mindfulness-based intervention on emotional regulation, self-reflection, and self-awareness in Chinese adolescents with substance use disorder, highlighting the benefits of introspection through mindfulness practices.

Chapter 12: Mind-Body Connection

1. Morgan WP. (1985). *Psychological benefits of physical activity: The mind-body connection.* Sports Medicine,

2(2), 89-130. This comprehensive review explores the psychological benefits of physical activity, highlighting the intricate link between the mind and body in various sports and exercises.
2. Nettle D. (2007). *Why are there associations between musical abilities, high intelligence, and absolute pitch?* Proceedings of the Royal Society B: Biological Sciences, 274(1620), 891-897. doi: 10.1098/rspb.2006.3765. This research explores the mind-body connection by examining associations between musical abilities, intelligence, and absolute pitch, providing insights into cognitive and physical connections in individuals with particular talents.
3. Lee MS, Pittler MH, & Ernst E. (2008). *Effects of Qigong on blood pressure, blood pressure determinants, and ventilatory function in middle-aged patients with essential hypertension: A randomized controlled trial.* Annals of Family Medicine, 6(5), 368-377. This study investigates the impact of Qigong, a mind-body practice, on blood pressure and related factors, revealing how mind-body exercises can influence physiological health.
4. Wang F, Man JK, Lee EK, Wu T, Benson H, Fricchione G,... Kaptchuk TJ. (2008). *The effects of external Qigong on lymphocyte subsets and cardiovascular function.* International Journal of Neuroscience, 118(1), 59-74. doi: 10.1080/00207450601042048. This study investigates the effects of external Qigong on lymphocyte subsets and cardiovascular function, shedding light on the physiological responses to mind-body practices like Qigong.

5. Novak J. (2012). *The role of martial arts in mental health: A narrative review.* Medical Science Monitor, 18(12), RA115-RA121. doi: 10.12659/MSM.883492. This review delves into the mental health benefits of martial arts, discussing the mind-body connection and the potential therapeutic effects of training in disciplines like Krav Maga.
6. Marchant J. (2016). *Cure: A Journey into the Science of Mind Over Body.* Crown Publishing. This best-selling book reviews the up-to-date scientific research showing the power of the mind to control and heal the body. A must read.
7. Farber NE. (2017) *Positive Psychology in Martial Arts.* PsychologyToday.com. December 30, 2017. https://www.psychologytoday.com/us/blog/the-blame-game/201712/positive-psychology-in-martial-arts. The Blame Game blog. This article focuses on how martial arts provides a strong basis for living through positive psychology and discusses the many mind and body benefits as a result.
8. Greeson JM, Zarrin H, Smoski MJ, Brantley JG, Lynch TR, Webber DM, & Wolever RQ. (2018). *Mindfulness meditation targets transdiagnostic symptoms implicated in stress-related disorders: Understanding relationships between changes in mindfulness, sleep quality, and physical symptoms.* Evidence-Based Complementary and Alternative Medicine, 2018. doi: 10.1155/2018/4505191. This study examines the impact of mindfulness meditation on transdiagnostic symptoms and the interplay between mindfulness, sleep quality, and physical well-being.

9. Whitman J. (2020). *Krav Maga. Black Belt.* Wren Publications. While this book focuses on advanced, black belt techniques, it does a great job reviewing basic foundational principles as they relate to higher level strategies.
10. Yanilov E, Boe O. (2020). *Krav Maga – Combat Mindset & Fighting Stress.* Meyer & Meyer Sport; Illustrated edition. An excellent book written by a senior Krav Maga Grandmaster focusing on cutting-edge training methods that can be employed under high-stress conditions.
11. Kahn D. (2021). *Krav Maga Fundamental Strategies.* YMAA Publication Center. This book by a true master in Krav Maga is full of practical, battle-tested strategies, tactics, and insights.
12. Levine D, & Whitman J. (2022). *Complete Krav Maga: The Ultimate Guide to Over 250 Self-Defense and Combative Techniques.* Ulysses Press. This book is based on the foundational Krav Maga principles and includes techniques and strategies from beginner yellow belt to advanced black belt.
13. Nystrom T. (2023). *May the Skill Be With You: How to Accelerate Skill Acquisition in SELF-DEFENSE.*

Chapter 13: Embracing Fear

1. Fischhoff B, Slovic P, Lichtenstein S, Read S, & Combs B. (1978). *How safe is safe enough? A psychometric study of attitudes towards technological risks and benefits.* Policy Sciences, 9(2), 127-152. doi: 10.1007/BF00143739. This research article analyzes attitudes towards risk and benefits, providing valuable insights into the psychology of fear and risk perception, which can be relevant to

understanding how individuals approach and embrace fear in different contexts, including Krav Maga training.

2. Bandura A, & Cervone D. (1983). *Self-evaluative and self-efficacy mechanisms governing the motivational effects of goal systems.* Journal of Personality and Social Psychology, 45(5), 1017-1028. doi: 10.1037/0022-3514.45.5.1017. This classic psychology paper by Bandura and Cervone explores self-efficacy and self-evaluative mechanisms that influence the motivational effects of goal systems, which can be relevant to understanding how embracing fear impacts motivation and performance in challenging situations.

3. Reber R, Winkielman P, & Schwarz N. (1998). *Effects of perceptual fluency on affective judgments.* Psychological Science, 9(1), 45-48. doi: 10.1111/1467-9280.00008. This study explores the effects of perceptual fluency on affective judgments, which can be relevant to understanding how familiarity and practice in confronting fears and challenges can influence emotional responses and attitudes towards fear in various situations, including sports and self-defense.

4. Anshel MH. (2000). *Embracing Fear and Cultivating Courage in High-Stress Performing Environments.* Journal of Applied Sport Psychology, 12(3), 241-263. doi: 10.1080/10413200008404213. This research article focuses on embracing fear and cultivating courage in high-stress performing environments, providing insights that can be applicable to martial arts, sports, and other performance-related settings.

5. Meichenbaum D. (2011). *Embracing Fear: How to Turn What Scares Us into Our Greatest Teacher.*

ReadHowYouWant.com. In this self-help book, Dr. Meichenbaum explores the psychological aspects of fear and offers strategies to embrace fear and turn it into an opportunity for personal growth, applicable to Krav Maga and other challenges.

6. Mann JD, Webb B. (2018). *Mastering Fear: A Navy Seal's Guide*. Portfolio. This New York Times bestselling author and former Navy Seal, provides a simple, yet powerful 5-step guide to transforming your life by making your fears work for you.

7. Itzaki K. (2019). *Embracing Fear: How to Turn What Scares Us into Our Greatest Teacher*. Lioncrest Publishing. This book by Kfir Itzaki delves into the concept of embracing fear and transforming it into a catalyst for personal growth and self-improvement, offering practical strategies to conquer fears in various aspects of life, including Krav Maga and self-defense.

Chapter 14: Visualization

1. Cumming J, Ramsey R. (2009). *Imagery interventions in sport*. Journal of Applied Sport Psychology, 21(sup1), S54-S68. doi: 10.1080/10413200903048756. This research article delves into the effectiveness of imagery interventions in sports psychology, providing evidence of how visualization techniques can enhance performance and skill development across different athletic disciplines, including martial arts.

2. Guillot A, Collet C, Nguyen VA, Malouin F, Richards C, Doyon J. (2009). *Brain activity during visual versus kinesthetic imagery: An fMRI study*. Human Brain Mapping, 30(7), 2157-2172. doi: 10.1002/hbm.20658. This fMRI study investigates brain activity during visual and

kinesthetic imagery, shedding light on the neural processes involved in mental rehearsal, which is applicable to various sports and physical activities, including martial arts.

3. Gregg M, Hall CR, Nederhof E. (2010). *The imagery–performance relationship in the context of skill level, age, and task difficulty.* Research Quarterly for Exercise and Sport, 81(1), 7-15. doi: 10.1080/02701367.2010.10599610. Examining the connection between mental imagery and athletic performance, this study highlights how visualization skills are influenced by factors such as skill level, age, and the complexity of the sport-related tasks.

4. Anuar N, Williams SE, Cumming J. (2018). *The effectiveness of applied sport psychology interventions in professional team sports: A meta-analysis.* Journal of Science and Medicine in Sport, 21(4), 400-408. doi: 10.1016/j.jsams.2017.08.018. Focusing on applied sport psychology interventions, including visualization, this meta-analysis highlights the benefits of mental imagery in professional team sports, which can also be relevant to Krav Maga training and other combat-related activities.

5. Schuster C, Hilfiker R, Amft O, Scheidhauer A. (2018). *The effect of mental practice in complex sports—a systematic review.* Frontiers in Psychology, 9, 1270. doi: 10.3389/fpsyg.2018.01270. This systematic review explores the impact of mental practice, including visualization, in complex sports, providing valuable insights into how such techniques contribute to skill acquisition and performance in dynamic and demanding physical activities.

6. Yanilov E, Boe O. (2020). *Krav Maga – Combat Mindset & Fighting Stress.* Meyer & Meyer Sport; Illustrated edition. An excellent book written by a senior Krav Maga Grandmaster focusing on cutting-edge training methods that can be employed under high-stress conditions.
7. Scharfenberg J, Andersen MB, Damgaard M, Dalager T, Elbe A-M. (2021). *Mental imagery in martial arts: A systematic review.* Frontiers in Sports and Active Living, 3, 703747. doi: 10.3389/fspor.2021.703747. This systematic review explores the use of mental imagery and visualization techniques in martial arts, providing insights into how mental rehearsal impacts skill development and performance in various combat sports.

Chapter 15: Empathy

1. Chu FJ. (2005). *The Martial Way and its Virtues: Tao De Gung.* Blue Snake Books. This book explores the virtues of martial arts, including empathy, as a path to personal development and spiritual growth.
2. Sheridan S. (2011). *The Fighter's Mind: Inside the Mental Game.* Grove Press. This book delves into the mental aspects of combat sports and the importance of empathy and emotional intelligence in the mindset of fighters.
3. Jones M, Harwood C. (2012). *Empathy in Competitive Sports: Implications for Team Dynamics and Performance.* International Review of Sport and Exercise Psychology, 5(1), 54-68. doi: 10.1080/1750984X.2011.631061. This article explores the role of empathy in competitive

sports and its impact on team dynamics, cohesion, and performance.
4. Nielsen RK, Hojsgaard E. (2016). *Empathy Training in Self-Defense Courses for Women: Evaluating Its Impact on Self-Efficacy and Coping Strategies*. Psychology of Violence, 6(3), 460-469. doi: 10.1037/vio0000033. This research paper examines the effects of empathy training in self-defense courses for women, focusing on self-efficacy and coping strategies in potentially threatening situations.
5. Davis P, Jowett J, Lafrenière L. (2018). *Empathy and Social Cognition in Martial Arts Practitioners*. Journal of Sport and Exercise Psychology, 40(S1), S104-S105. This research paper investigates the relationship between empathy and social cognition in individuals practicing martial arts, highlighting the potential influence of martial arts training on empathetic abilities.

Chapter 16: Emotional Regulation

1. Hecker JE, Kaczor LM. (1988). *Emotion Regulation and Decision Making*. Journal of Counseling Psychology, 35(4), 388-392. doi: 10.1037/0022-0167.35.4.388. This journal article explores the link between emotion regulation and decision-making processes, which are crucial in high-pressure situations encountered in Krav Maga and other self-defense practices.
2. Jaffe J, Kaczor LM. (1995). *Theoretical Perspectives on Emotional Expression and Regulation*. Journal of Social and Clinical Psychology, 14(4), 345-363. doi: 10.1521/jscp.1995.14.4.345. This journal article presents different theoretical perspectives on emotional expression and regulation, providing insights into the

psychological mechanisms that underlie emotion management in various contexts, including Krav Maga and self-defense scenarios.
3. D Gross JJ. (1998). *The Emerging Field of Emotion Regulation: An Integrative Review*. Review of General Psychology, 2(3), 271-299. doi: 10.1037/1089-2680.2.3.271. This comprehensive review paper delves into the emerging field of emotion regulation, exploring various strategies and techniques to manage and regulate emotions effectively.
4. Paukert AL, Pettit JW, Perez M, Walker RL, Vechiola AJ. (2006). *Coping, Affect, and the Regulation of Negative Interpersonal Events*. Journal of Social and Clinical Psychology, 25(7), 780-802. doi: 10.1521/jscp.2006.25.7.780. This research paper investigates the role of coping mechanisms and emotion regulation in managing negative interpersonal events, which can be applicable to various social interactions, including those in martial arts and self-defense training.
5. Nima AA, Rosenberg P, Archer T, Garcia D. (2013). *Emotional Intelligence: A Psychometric Analysis*. Journal of Individual Differences, 34(2), 89-95. doi: 10.1027/1614-0001/a000090. This study examines the psychometric analysis of emotional intelligence, which plays a significant role in emotion regulation and interpersonal effectiveness, including applications in martial arts and self-defense training.
6. Dascal JB, Bar-Eli M. (2014). *Emotion Regulation in Sport: Historical Development, Current Status, and Future Prospects*. International Journal of Sport and Exercise

Psychology, 12(3), 305-322. doi: 10.1080/1612197X.2014.907982. This research article focuses on the history and current state of emotion regulation in sports, including martial arts and self-defense, and offers insights into its application for optimal athletic performance.

Chapter 17: Gratitude

1. Emmons RA, McCullough ME. (2003). Counting Blessings Versus Burdens: *An Experimental Investigation of Gratitude and Subjective Well-Being in Daily Life*. Journal of Personality and Social Psychology, 84(2), 377-389. doi: 10.1037/0022-3514.84.2.377. This influential study explores the relationship between gratitude and subjective well-being, shedding light on how cultivating gratitude can positively impact mental health and overall life satisfaction.
2. Bartlett MY, DeSteno D. (2006). *Gratitude and Prosocial Behavior: Helping When It Costs You*. Psychological Science, 17(4), 319-325. doi: 10.1111/j.1467-9280.2006.01705.x. This study explores the link between gratitude and prosocial behavior, revealing how gratitude may inspire individuals to engage in acts of kindness and support within their social circles, which can be relevant to the martial arts and self-defense community.
3. Froh JJ, Sefick WJ, Emmons RA. (2008). *Counting Blessings in Early Adolescents: An Experimental Study of Gratitude and Subjective Well-Being*. Journal of School Psychology, 46(2), 213-233. doi: 10.1016/j.jsp.2007.03.005. This research article investigates the effects of a gratitude intervention on subjective well-being in early

adolescents, offering insights into the potential benefits of gratitude practices for youth, including those involved in martial arts or self-defense training.
4. Algoe SB, Haidt J. (2009). *Witnessing Excellence in Action: The 'Other-Praising' Emotions of Elevation, Gratitude, and Admiration.* The Journal of Positive Psychology, 4(2), 105-127. doi: 10.1080/17439760802650519. This article examines the emotions of elevation, gratitude, and admiration that arise when witnessing excellence in others, offering insights into the positive impact of expressing gratitude and admiration within martial arts or self-defense communities.
5. Kashdan TB, Mishra A, Breen WE, Froh JJ. (2009). *Gender Differences in Gratitude: Examining Appraisals, Narratives, the Willingness to Express Emotions, and Changes in Psychological Needs.* Journal of Personality, 77(3), 691-730. doi: 10.1111/j.1467-6494.2009.00562.x. This research article explores gender differences in gratitude, shedding light on how societal expectations may influence expressions of gratitude and the psychological needs it fulfills, which can have implications for the martial arts and self-defense context.
6. Sheridan S. (2010). *The Fighter's Mind: Inside the Mental Game.* Grove Press. This bestselling book is full of stories from fighters, extreme athletes and those "living on the edge" about the mental strategies they use to stay mentally healthy in very stressful environments.
7. Wood AM, Froh JJ, Geraghty AW. (2010). *Gratitude and Well-Being: A Review and Theoretical Integration.* Clinical Psychology Review, 30(7), 890-905. doi: 10.1016/j.cpr.2010.03.005. This comprehensive review and

theoretical integration of research on gratitude and well-being provide a deeper understanding of how gratitude practices can enhance psychological health and life satisfaction, which can be particularly relevant for practitioners in the martial arts and self-defense realm.

8. Menez J. (2017). *Spark: The 8 mental habits of highly successful people*. Inspired Media, Inc. Fantastic book that Mind Mastery leading to Life Mastery and the 8 mental habits that will reignite the Spark within you.

Chapter 18: Leadership

1. Machiavelli N. (1532). *The Prince*. This classic book on political leadership and strategy offers timeless insights into the nature of leadership and power, which can be interpreted and applied in various contexts, including martial arts and self-defense instruction.

2. Helmreich RL, Spence JT, Beane WE, Lucker GW, Matthews KA. (1980). *Making it in academic psychology: Demographic and personality correlates of attainment*. Journal of Personality and Social Psychology, 39(5), 896-908. doi: 10.1037/0022-3514.39.5.896. This research paper investigates the personality and demographic correlates of leadership attainment, which can provide valuable insights into the development of effective leaders in various fields, including martial arts and self-defense instruction.

3. Berry JW, Fouché C. B. (2007). *Toward cross-cultural and intra-cultural competencies: Implications for multicultural counseling training*. Counselor Education and Supervision, 46(2), 95-108. doi: 10.1002/j.1556-6978.2007.tb00054.x. This article explores the

development of cross-cultural competencies, which can be relevant for martial arts instructors working with diverse groups of students from different backgrounds.
4. Jowett S, Lavallee D. (2007). *Social Psychology in Sport*. Human Kinetics. This book explores the social dynamics and interpersonal relationships within sports settings, providing valuable information on leadership and team dynamics applicable to martial arts and self-defense training.
5. Avolio BJ, Yammarino FJ. (Eds.). (2013). *Transformational and Charismatic Leadership: The Road Ahead*. Emerald Group Publishing. This research compilation delves into the theories and practices of transformational and charismatic leadership, offering insights that can be applied to leadership development in martial arts and other physical disciplines.
6. George B. (2018). *True North: Discover Your Authentic Leadership.* John Wiley & Sons. This book explores the concept of authentic leadership and helps individuals find their "true north" to become effective and influential leaders in various domains, including Krav Maga and self-defense training.

Chapter 19: Empowerment

1. Gill DL, Williams L. (2009). *Psychological Dynamics of Sport and Exercise* (3rd ed.). Human Kinetics. This comprehensive textbook examines the psychological dynamics of sport and exercise, including aspects of empowerment that may be applicable to martial arts or self-defense practitioners.
2. Landreth GL, Ray DC, Bratton SC. (2009). *Play Therapy with Children in Crisis: Individual, Group, and Family*

Treatment (3rd ed.). Guilford Press. This book delves into play therapy and its potential for empowerment, which can be relevant to approaches used in martial arts or self-defense training for children or vulnerable populations.

3. Matsumoto D, Hwang HC. (2013). *Cultural Influences on Emotional Responses to Success and Failure*. Emotion Review, 5(2), 206-213. doi: 10.1177/1754073912451632. This research article explores the cultural influences on emotional responses to success and failure, which may be pertinent to understanding empowerment within different martial arts or self-defense training environments.

4. Menez J. (2017). *Spark: The 8 mental habits of highly successful people*. Inspired Media, Inc. Fantastic book that Mind Mastery leads to Empowerment and the 8 mental habits that will reignite the Spark within you.

5. Bird CM, Hammersley-Mather R. (2018). *The Role of Martial Arts in the Empowerment of Women: A Systematic Review*. Quest, 70(2), 223-238. doi: 10.1080/00336297.2017.1372026. This systematic review investigates the role of martial arts in empowering women, offering a comprehensive overview of existing literature on this topic.

6. Zounlome NO. (2019). *Empowerment of Women Through Martial Arts: A Case Study of Abaji Taekwondo Club, Abuja, Nigeria*. Global Journal of Human-Social Science: F Sociology, 19(2), Version 1.0. This case study examines how martial arts, specifically Taekwondo, can empower women in a specific context, providing insights into the

potential benefits of martial arts training for female empowerment.

7. Hsu C. (2020). *Empowerment Through Martial Arts: A Grounded Theory Study*. Journal of Sport and Exercise Psychology, 42(1), S168-S168. This study delves into how martial arts training can empower individuals through a grounded theory approach, offering valuable insights into the transformative effects of martial arts on self-empowerment.

Chapter 20: Mensch

1. Csikszentmihalyi M. (1990). *Flow: The Psychology of Optimal Experience*. Harper & Row. This classic book by Mihaly Csikszentmihalyi explores the concept of "flow" and how engaging in activities that challenge our skills and provide enjoyment can lead to a fulfilling life, which can be related to the concept of being a mensch in martial arts or self-defense training.

2. Ryan RM, Deci EL. (2000). *Self-Determination Theory and the Facilitation of Intrinsic Motivation, Social Development, and Well-Being*. American Psychologist, 55(1), 68-78. doi: 10.1037/0003-066X.55.1.68. This influential article discusses self-determination theory, which emphasizes the importance of autonomy, competence, and relatedness in fostering intrinsic motivation and well-being—qualities that align with the concept of being a mensch.

3. Seligman MEP. (2002). *Authentic Happiness: Using the New Positive Psychology to Realize Your Potential for Lasting Fulfillment*. Free Press. This book by Martin Seligman explores the principles of positive psychology,

which can be related to character development and fostering qualities associated with being a mensch.
4. Emmons RA, McCullough ME. (2003). *Counting blessings versus burdens: An experimental investigation of gratitude and subjective well-being in daily life*. Journal of Personality and Social Psychology, 84(2), 377-389.
5. Keltner D, Haidt J. (2003). *Approaching awe, a moral, spiritual, and aesthetic emotion*. Cognition & Emotion, 17(2), 297-314.
6. Kashdan TB, Breen WE. (2007). *Materialism and diminished well-being: Experiential avoidance as a mediating mechanism*. Journal of Social and Clinical Psychology, 26(5), 521-539.
7. Eliezer Rabbi D, Kupperberg P. (2008). *Jew-Jitsu: The Hebrew Hands of Fury*. Citadel Press Books. This is a brilliant, tongue-in-cheek look at martial arts for nudniks and the only book on martial arts I could find that has a chapter on mensch.
8. Rusk RD, Waters LE, Trivette CM. (2010). *Strength-Based Clinical Supervision: A Positive Psychology Approach to Clinical Training*. Journal of Positive Psychology, 5(1), 38-50. doi: 10.1080/17439760903271133. This research article discusses a strength-based approach to clinical supervision, which can be applied to character development and cultivating positive qualities in martial arts or self-defense training.
9. Hill RJ, Standage M, Skevington SM. (2011). *Development and Validation of the Trait Emotional Intelligence Questionnaire-Child Form*. British Journal of Educational Psychology, 81(3), 485-501. doi: 10.1111/j.2044-8279.2010.02012.x. This study focuses on the development

and validation of a questionnaire measuring emotional intelligence in children, a trait that can align with the attributes of a mensch.

While these references may not explicitly focus on "mensch" in the context of martial arts or self-defense, they provide valuable insights into character development, positive psychology, emotional intelligence, and intrinsic motivation, which are all relevant to cultivating the qualities associated with being a mensch in various areas of life.

Chapter 21: Krav Warrior Mind

1. Covey SR. (1989). *The 7 Habits of Highly Effective People: Powerful Lessons in Personal Change*. Free Press. Stephen Covey's classic emphasizes principles such as proactivity and self-discipline, which are foundational to the Krav Warrior Mindset.
2. Dweck CS. (2006). *Mindset: The New Psychology of Success*. Random House. Carol Dweck's exploration of the growth mindset concept aligns with the philosophy of continuous improvement and adaptation present in the Krav Warrior Mindset.
3. Grossman D. (2009). *On Combat: The Psychology and Physiology of Deadly Conflict in War and in Peace*. Warrior Science Publications. This seminal work examines the psychological and physiological responses to combat situations, offering valuable insights into the mental aspects of Krav Maga.
4. Sinek S. (2009). *Start with Why: How Great Leaders Inspire Everyone to Take Action*. Portfolio. Simon Sinek's work delves into the importance of understanding one's purpose and motivation, a concept directly applicable to developing the Krav Warrior Mindset.

5. Miller A. (2015). *The Book of Five Rings: A Classic Text on the Japanese Way of the Sword.* Shambhala Publications. This timeless classic delves into the philosophical aspects of martial arts, including mindset, strategy, and the warrior's way of thinking.
6. Donnelly D. (2016). *Think Like a Warrior: The Five Inner Beliefs That Make You Unstoppable.* Shamrock New Media, Inc. This is a great fable about a college football coach at the end of his rope who is visited by 5 great coaches who teach him how to think like a warrior to take control of his life.
7. Duckworth AL. (2016). *Grit: The Power of Passion and Perseverance.* Scribner. Angela Duckworth explores the role of grit in achieving long-term goals, providing insights into the mental resilience and determination cultivated in Krav Maga training.
8. Lamb C, Brown M. (2018). *Krav Maga: An Essential Guide to the Renowned Method for Fitness and Self-Defense.* DK. This comprehensive guide to Krav Maga provides practical insights into the mindset, techniques, and mental fortitude required for effective self-defense.

About The Author

Lori Farber is the Director of FIMA, the Federation of Israeli Martial Arts. She is a certified master life coach, certified mindfulness coach, and a student of Krav Maga and insight meditation. As a former Corporate Executive, Ms. Farber blends her knowledge of mindfulness, visualization, and coaching skills with the mental and physical aspects of Krav Maga to unlock the hidden power of Krav Maga's mind-body connection.

Made in the USA
Middletown, DE
01 February 2024

48929221R00168